BIBLE VERSES GIVEN TO ME:

A MEMOIR

Jo A. Baldwin

AMEC Sunday School Union
Nashville

To

The Right Reverend Carolyn Tyler Guidry

A Splendid Bishop

CONTENTS

ACKNOWLEDGMENTS

I would like to express my appreciation to the African Methodist Episcopal churches I gratefully served as pastor: Featherston Chapel and St. Paul in Senatobia, Mississippi, two part-time mission churches in the Eighth Episcopal District that I was appointed to by The Right Reverend Cornal Garnett Henning, Sr.; Greater Disney Chapel, a full-time station church in Greenville, Mississippi, that I was promoted and appointed to by The Right Reverend Carolyn Tyler Guidry—to whom this book is dedicated—and now Kosciusko AME Church, "A New Work" Bishop Guidry appointed me to making me an apostle who is— among other things—a person who starts churches. The congregations are loving and supportive of my ministry and give me feedback on my sermons and Bible Study lessons that assist me greatly in my writings.

I am thankful to Presiding Elder J. W. Hilton, Jr., of the South Mississippi Conference for teaching me step-by-step what to do when I enter a church house as the pastor, and Presiding Elder Archie R. Smith of the North Mississippi Conference for his intellectual support.

I am grateful with all my heart to Dr. Johnny Barbour, Jr., President/Publisher of the AME Church Sunday School Union, for publishing my book.

And, I would be remiss if I did not say how much I sincerely appreciate Mr. Audrey Ball of Friendship AME Church in Clarksdale, for allowing me to sit in his Men's Sunday School class every year at Conference to hear him superbly exegete Scripture, and Mr. James Otis Watson of Mount Ora AME Church in Grenada—who is a master builder—for designing and building our beautiful altar rail and pulpit prayer bench for Kosciusko AME Church, where I pastor.

I honor the memory of Mr. James Strange, my paternal grandparents' friend in Covington, Tennessee, who called me Jochebed when I was a little girl. I did not know that was the name of Moses' mother (see Num. 26:59) until I read the Bible cover-to-cover for the first time when I was fourteen.

One person who began helping me back in 1998 is the late Rev. George Witmer. He was a charismatic Presbyterian (U.S.A.) minister. Rev. Witmer invited me to preach at his church that year and since then his wife, Virginia, and he became good friends of mine. Virginia died in 2006 and Rev. Witmer in October 2007.

Rev. Witmer had a Prayer Language that yielded prophecies. We were prayer partners and he started receiving prophetic messages for me over the course of four years that he would type on index cards and mail me. I have included all seven from the first in 1998 to the last in 2001, so readers can see how my special personal verses were predicted years before I received them.

> 11/08/1998
>
> If you have faith as small as a mustard seed, you will accomplish the moving of mountains. Nothing will be impossible to you, if you step out by faith! (Matt. 17:20)
>
> God is going to strengthen you with power through His Holy Spirit in your inner being, so that Christ may dwell in your heart through faith (Eph. 3:16, 17) so you may be filled with all the fullness of God. So, begin to ask God to pour out His Spirit and His power upon His people.
>
> Now that the Holy Spirit has revealed Himself, let all hearts know that the Holy Spirit has spoken GOD'S WORD TO YOU.
>
> 03/22/1999
>
> Let us listen (hearken) to the words of the Lord so we may come alive to the faith of the Church. If you have faith as small as a mustard seed, you will be able to move mountains and do the

impossible. Listen to the words of the Lord with ears that hear so you may have new life in His Spirit. So seek new life in His Spirit. For God has called you to proclaim the acceptable year of the Lord and the day of God's judgment, so you can comfort those who mourn: To those who mourn, you are to give them beauty for ashes; the oil of joy for mourning and the garment of praise for the spirit of heaviness. (Isa. 61:2, 3)

05/23/1999

Behold saith the Lord, you are my servant, for I have called you to minister in My name. You shall know My power and the leading of My Spirit, for I shall bear witness with your heart in this work I have called you to do. Be encouraged as My disciple for your own faith shall be strengthened. Hearts shall be touched. Healings will take place and lives shall be transformed. You shall be encouraged by My Spirit for I will accomplish this work through you.

"These signs shall follow those who believe: In My name shall they cast out devils; they shall speak with new tongues; they shall lay hands on the sick and they shall recover" (Mk. 16:17, 18).

09/10/1999

Hear these words now, saith the Spirit of God, for I go before you with grace and power in My name for healing in the name of Jesus! Hallelujah! Praise God! Praise God for His healing power! Rejoice in the gift of healing which has been placed in your hands. Honor the Father, the Son and the Holy Spirit and follow the Biblical guidelines for the anointing with oil in the name of Jesus (Jas. 5:14), for this honors the Father, the Son and the Holy Spirit. Go forth as My servant now to the work I have called you. Be wary of those who would try to detract you from doing the will of the Father. Be more alert to the strategy of the enemy as you do the work of the Kingdom. Amen. 5:00 P.M.

07/17/2000

(Remember these words my son, for My heart has been open to your prayers. You shall receive the answer to your prayers, especially for My servant. This is what you should say:)

"Listen, my child, for I have heard your prayers. New doors of opportunity will soon be open for you. You shall hear My voice and follow My direction. You will know which way you should turn when you follow My direction. This leading of My Spirit will come to you very soon. You shall receive confirmation very soon regarding new and open doors for new ways of ministry." 11:22 P.M.

06/17/2001

Behold, my daughter, I have called you to be My prophet. You have heard My call and are walking in the ways I have led you. Let these words guide you in order to walk in the ways of My Kingdom: Think of what you were when you were called (see 1 Cor. 1:26). "God has chosen the foolish things of the world to confound the wise and He has chosen the weak things of the world to confound the strong" (1 Cor. 1:27). Because you are lifting up My Son, Jesus, people will be drawn from the east and the west to hear the words of faith and to discover how to walk by faith. Be faithful, my daughter, to your call of ministry and let your call be your guide in the way you follow my direction. Remember the Cross and what the Cross represents in your life as you follow the ways of the kingdom, even as I have called you (see 1 Cor. 1:2-31). Amen. 7:30 P.M.

10/16/2001

Behold, My servant, I have called you to be My prophet. You have heard this call in your heart. The time has come for you to listen to my Words in a new way. For behold, I am about to do a new thing. Give yourself to My Word through My Spirit, saith the Lord, for a new Word will be given to you to proclaim to My people. You shall hear My Word and declare that Word as My prophet. Search your heart, now, saith the Lord and learn of new doors which will be open to you. For you shall go forth with a new authority and a new power to proclaim My Word to My people. For I am about to do a new thing through you, saith the Lord. Amen. (see Ps. 62 and Ps. 63)

After receiving Rev. Witmer's last prophecy, he sent me John 14:27: "Peace I leave with you, My peace I give to you; not as the world gives do I give to you. Let not your heart be troubled, neither let it be afraid." He reminded me of the Holy Spirit's greatest role, that of Comforter (see Jn. 16:7). We are comforted when we are healed, when our children are doing well, when our bills are paid, when our prayers are answered, when we can rest. But to me the best comfort is having peace of mind. I appreciate Rev. Witmer's wisdom and friendship.

And again I thank the Father, Son, and Holy Ghost whose name is Jesus.

FOREWORD TO
REVEREND DR. BALDWIN'S MEMOIR

Dr. Jo Baldwin's memoir showed me an interesting way to look at certain passages in the Bible on the Godhead in particular.

There comes a time when an individual will look at a few old and worn words and a new revelation is seen and a new conversation is begun. This new conversation breaks ground that has been walked on many times before which creates a pathway for those who are walking to watch each footstep because they may miss some stone that has not been seen. Dr. Baldwin is creating a new conversation that those who read this work must engage in. This conversation begins with a look at Jesus and who He is, what He accomplished with His death and resurrection and how these two events impact the lives of those who accept and believe in Him.

The words of God are written so that the Word of God can be seen, handled, understood and then shared with others who also need to understand the power of Jesus that can always be found in the words He speaks. Those times when it appears that code is being used by Jesus, Paul and other writers of the scriptures reinforces the idea that it takes the revelation of the Holy Spirit to understand the things of God. Without this understanding being provided by the LORD Himself, the words will appear to be foolish words, spoken by foolish people and only understood by fools.

Any new conversation will have those who will agree and disagree. These two sides coming together in the spirit of discovery form the path Dr. Baldwin has created for those of us who study the scriptures to follow. She mentions certain passages that explain the Trinity as thought, word and deed. It is clear that every deed is the result of a word spoken and every word spoken, whether it is out loud or to oneself, is the direct result of a thought. The Trinity, long misunderstood, can begin to gain a clear understanding when the steps of a thought leading to a word, leading to a deed is grasped by those who are seeking a closer relationship with the Father, the Son and the Holy Spirit.

The trinity of thought, word and deed will lead an individual to question what he or she believes and how that belief system under-girds one's own thoughts, words and deeds. As this book challenges an individual to take part in a new conversation, it also will challenge a person to look at the scriptures with a new eye for seeing and a new mind for understanding. New and open conversations always lead to discovery and it is discovery that will lead a person to a new understanding and a closer relationship with God the Father, Jesus the Son and the Holy Spirit.

As you read this work, allow the Spirit to open the trinity of your thoughts and words to lead you to new deeds that can and will impact your growth and the growth of those whose lives you may touch.

L. Anthony Gatewood, Th.D.
Presiding Elder of
The African Methodist Episcopal Church
Third Episcopal District
Columbus, OH

PREFACE

The inspiration to write my memoir did not come until 2005, although I had been writing down certain verses in a notebook for more than nine years prior to that. It started when I read in the Old Testament where God spoke to Abram telling him to leave his father's house and go to a land he would show him. I saw that when Abram asked God where he was going, God in essence said, "I'll tell you later." Abram obeyed and took his wife and nephew along with his personal household and started on the journey (see Gen. 12:1-9). I saw that evidently when God calls someone to do a certain thing, a covenant starts right then. And when the person obeys God and does what he or she is called to do, the covenant is established. Such is the case with me. I was led to write down in a notebook Bible verses and passages that stood out to me and see what messages came out of them for me. So over the years I have gathered many personal verses I would like to share and tell what I think they mean.

I have read translated versions of the Bible cover-to-cover over nine times and have a Prayer Language that the Lord gave me many years ago that helps me get an understanding of the Scriptures directly from the Holy Ghost who is doing the praying through me.

For those who do not know, a Prayer Language is speaking in tongues. I remember asking for the gift when watching an Oral Roberts television show back in the 1980s. Shortly after asking, the Holy Ghost gave me the following list of some of his names to "prime the pump" for the language I would get: Yahweh (Bryant 610), Adonai (Bryant 610), Elohim (Gen. 1:1), El Shaddai (Gen. 17:1), Jehovah (Ex. 17:15), Jesus (Lk. 1:31), and Word (Rev. 19:13). The Spirit told me to say his names over and over again as fast as I could until my spontaneous utterance emerged. That is what I did, and that is what happened.

I have only spoken in tongues in public worship one time and there was a woman interpreter present who said my tongues spoke of a child I knew who was

1

in trouble. Shortly afterwards, I was told by a seminary classmate friend of mine that her daughter who was still in high school was pregnant.

Richard Foster, in his book *Prayer: Finding the Heart's True Home*, describes my experience accurately. He says *rhema* means word/revelation in Greek and that speaking in tongues or *glossolalia* is a Prayer of the Heart (137). He goes on to say that, "*glossolalia* is a release of our spirit into the Spirit of God whereby the Spirit prays through us. Spirit touches spirit [and] we enter the heavenlies by means of a heavenly language ... also called 'prayer language'" (138), and I have found that to be true of me. I feel like God is talking to himself out loud through me making my prayers second-hand. And I feel humbled and grateful that the Lord trusts me with the gift and uses me to pray for others. I feel restful during and after speaking in tongues and can pray in the spirit in a prayer service for two to three hours and not feel tired at the end.

So to begin sharing my verses I want to start by saying people are born into families and most can understand the relationship of mother-father-children. Parents love their offspring who are bone of their bones and flesh of their flesh (see Gen. 2:23). Babies are cared for and are a source of delight when growing up saying their first words, taking their first steps, laughing, learning and exploring. People understand that kind of love.

Jesus had parents. His mother's name was Mary and she was married to a man named Joseph, who was a carpenter. The Bible only speaks about Jesus' childhood when he was twelve years old. He seemingly got lost in Jerusalem when the family went there for Passover and were on their way home. Mary and Joseph had to go back to look for him and found him in the temple speaking with the leaders (see Lk. 2:41-52). Their fear turned to relief when they found him, but implied in the passage is that Jesus was yelled at and put on punishment for causing his parents to worry and inconveniencing them. They lost a day's journey going back to Jerusalem and spent three days there before they found him.

The Word is silent about Jesus until he is baptized (see Mt. 3:13-17) and begins his ministry. Families realize that children grow up and leave home. Most parents are sad but proud. People understand that kind of love.

However, if a young adult like Jesus—who is fully God too—goes from place-to-place teaching a new doctrine, performing miracles, healing the sick, restoring sight to the blind, casting out demons and even raising the dead, it is sure that his actions will raise a few eyebrows. But when he offends high-ranking Jews with statements he refuses to take back and upsets the money system in places like the temple and a pig farm, and allows all kinds of people of questionable character to follow him, and gets in big trouble from publicly talking with women, and working on the Sabbath and from being falsely accused, and goes to court and gets lied on and gets beaten to within an inch of his life and gets condemned to death by crucifixion, and suffers on a cross between two thieves, and cries forgiveness to his tormentors, and gives up the ghost and dies for the sins of the world, people cannot understand that kind of love.

So different theories about Jesus emerged, the prevailing one for Christians being he rose from the dead, because he was seen by people for forty days after his death (Acts 1:3) and was seen ascending into heaven (see Acts 1:9-11). Another theory is that his body was stolen and stories about his resurrection from the dead are not true (Mt. 27:63-65). But be that as it may because Jesus says, "the gates of hell shall not prevail against [his church]" (Mt. 16:18), it gets established.

Time passes and denominations come out of disagreements over doctrines except the African Methodist Episcopal Church (AME) of which I am a member. The AME Church was started as a protest to racial injustice. Black slaves were pulled off their knees while praying at the altar in St. George Methodist Church in Philadelphia, Pennsylvania, back in 1787. Richard Allen and others left that particular white church promising never to return because of the mistreatment and in 1816 organized the first black connectional Methodist Church in the United States (see Wright 5-6), but back to my main point.

3

People are still searching for truths about God to believe. In the meantime Jesus is concerned about his Word being misinterpreted and people being taught misconceptions about him. All of us need to be heard and it started with God, since we are created in his image. Perhaps one reason humans were made was so God could have more than himself to talk to like when he said, "Let us make man in our image after our likeness" (Gen. 1:26) at creation. Jesus also wants to be recognized when he comes again. Even though he has revealed to the Apostle John in the Book of Revelation how he will look when he comes back (see Rev. 19:11-16) and how the new heaven and the new earth will be through the analogy of the New Jerusalem (see Rev. 21:1-27), Jesus told me he is troubled by the distinction still being made in the Godhead. So he told me a few things to write down to stop me from dividing him into separate parts since his resurrection from the dead.

God says in his Word that he put on flesh in order to come to earth to die for the sins of the world. He called his flesh Son and named his flesh Jesus that means Savior. Those who believe God cannot die are mistaken, because his flesh could die and did. But for Christians, the main point to remember is that his flesh did not stay dead but a couple of days. Jesus rose from the dead on the third morning (see Mk. 16:1-8). People saw him (Mk. 16:9), talked with him (Lk. 24:13-31), ate with him (Jn. 21:1-15), touched him (Jn. 20:24-29) and saw him ascend into heaven (Acts 1:9). The Bible is my primary source, and I am to explain the verses given to me in such a way that even a child can understand.

INTRODUCTION

"He who forms the mountains, creates the wind, and reveals his thoughts to [humankind]" (Amos 4:13) said this to me: The distinction made in the Godhead during the Incarnation no longer applies. God deferred to his *spoken* Word after the Resurrection.

The Lord our God is <u>one</u> (Mk. 12:29). JESUS *was* the flesh of God when he walked the earth (Jn. 1:14). He *is* the Word of I AM THAT I AM who called the world into existence, whose Holy Spirit—his breath, sound, touch, and invisible body—moved upon the face of the waters (Gen. 1:2) calling "those things which be not as though they were" (Rom. 4:17).

"God said to Moses, I AM THAT I AM: and he said, Thus shalt thou say to the children of Israel, I AM hath sent me to you" (Ex. 3:14). "Jesus said to [the Pharisees], Truly, truly I say to you, Before Abraham was, I AM" (Jn. 8:58). Jesus said, "He who has seen me has seen the Father" (Jn. 14:9). "The Father and I are one" (Jn. 10:30).

The Incarnation means Jesus condescended to put on flesh and come to earth as a "holy thing" (Lk. 1:35) born of a woman, to die for the sins of the world. He walked the earth doing good (Acts 10:38) but taught a strange doctrine religious leaders rejected that says he is "equal with God" (Jn. 5:18). He was put on trial and falsely accused (Mk. 14:59). Pontius Pilate sentenced him to death by crucifixion (Lk. 23:23-24). He suffered on a cross and gave up the ghost (Jn. 19:30) and was buried in a new tomb (Mt. 27:60). On the third morning he rose from the dead (Mk. 16:2) and said to his disciples that he has "all power in heaven and on earth" (Mt. 28:18). He ascended into heaven going back to pure Spirit because "He that descended is the same also that ascended up far above all heavens, that he might fill all things" (Eph. 4:10).

Jesus is God, the Word made flesh (Jn. 1:14), the articulation of divine thought (see Ps. 29), "the power of God, and the wisdom of God" (1 Cor. 1:24), "the true God, and eternal life" (1 Jn. 5:20).

CHAPTER 1

"Who has gone up to heaven and come down? Who has gathered up the wind in the hollow of his hands? Who has wrapped up the waters in his cloak? Who has established the ends of the earth? What is his name? ... Tell me if you know!" (Prov. 30:4).

Jesus is God, the Word made flesh (Jn. 1:14), who rose from the dead with all power (Mt. 28:18).

Jesus was before the foundation of the world (see Jn. 17:24) and is the reason for creation. "In the beginning God created the heaven and the earth. And the earth was without form, and void; and darkness was upon the face of the deep. And the Spirit of God moved upon the face of the waters. And God said, Let there be light" (Gen. 1:1-3a) four days before he made the sun, because at creation Jesus was calling himself into visibility as the light of the world (Jn. 8:12).

God created the world by speaking the world into existence. When God uttered sound—the "Big Bang," if you will—Jesus was begotten, meaning caused or produced.

God was all pure Spirit before he made the decision to become a man and call his name Jesus. And he is all pure Spirit again since his ascension into heaven. Immediately after Jesus rose from the dead he was still flesh because the morning of his resurrection he told Mary Magdalene not to touch him because he had not yet ascended back to heaven (Jn. 20:17). And when Jesus came through a wall in the upper room where his disciples were hiding, he told doubting Thomas to feel the nail prints in his hands and thrust his hand into the wound in his side where he had been pierced when hanging on the cross. Jesus said to him, "A spirit hath not flesh and bones as you see me have" (Lk. 24:39).

Jesus also ate with people. When he was walking with Cleophas and his companion on the road to Emmaus and they invited him to go home with them saying "the day was far spent" (Lk. 24:29), as they were at the table, he broke the bread and vanished from their sight, and it was then that they realized who he was (Lk. 24:30-31).

Jesus also ate with Peter and some other disciples on the beach the morning after they had been fishing all night (Jn. 21:12, 15). So for forty days after his resurrection he was both spirit and flesh but since his ascension he is back to being pure Spirit again. Believers in Jesus are the flesh of God today.

When creating the world, God's first creation was light. God did not have to create darkness because before creation God dwelt in darkness and swirling water. "The Lord said that he would dwell in the thick darkness" (1 Kin. 8:12).

Darkness is good because before creation God spent time thinking in the darkness. This must be so since the plan of salvation was built into creation. Jesus was begotten when God spoke his thoughts—which are words—out loud. Jesus is the voice of God and the words spoken. Exodus 19:19 reads, "When the voice of the trumpet sounded long, and waxed louder and louder, Moses spake, and God answered him by a voice." "The voice of the Lord is upon the waters" (Ps. 29:3a). "The voice of the Lord is powerful … [and] full of majesty" (Ps. 29:4). "The voice of the Lord divideth the flames of fire" (Ps. 29:7). "The voice of the Lord shaketh the wilderness" (Ps. 29:8a). These verses show that the Word is the power of God because it is God's spoken words and not his thoughts that bring about creative action. There was action in the swirling water before the world was but it was not creative. It was indwelling action for God only. Creative action expands God and is beneficial to more than just God.

Jesus, the Word and voice of God, did the work of creation. The Bible says, "In the beginning was the Word, and the Word was with God, and the Word was God. The same was in the beginning with God. All things were made by him; and without him was not any thing made that was made. In him was life; and the life was the light of men. And the light shineth in darkness; and the darkness comprehended it not" (Jn. 1:1-5). This means that after the sounding of the Word the first appearance of Jesus was light. Saying, "Let there be light," Jesus was calling himself into visibility prior to his incarnation. Jesus has always

7

been visible since creation. He says in John 8:12, "I am the light of the world," which includes all light from all stars. And in the New Jerusalem, when he comes again, there will be no more need of the sun for the Lord will give the light (see Rev. 22:5).

CHAPTER 2

When I received the verses that told me God is "thought, Word and deed" and that I should share them with people, I asked the Lord, "Why me?" His answer was, "I have made you a watchman to the house of Israel: therefore hear the word at my mouth, and give them warning from me" (Ez. 3:17; 33:7). "Warning of what?" was my next question. The Spirit said I am tired of people misinterpreting the Scriptures, subordinating me because of the incarnation and not emphasizing enough the power of the resurrection. I need people to know that "all power" (Mt. 28:18) means just that. I am the Eternal God with all power in heaven and on earth. I called myself the Son of Man and the Son of God so people could begin to somewhat understand my relationship with myself and my relationship with them. Before I put on flesh it was impossible to know me or even see my face and live (Ex. 33:20). The most a person could see was my back (Ex. 33:23). I mainly appeared in signs and wonders like a pillar of cloud by day and a pillar of fire by night (Ex. 13:21). My voice was heard in thunder and lightning (Ex. 20:18-19) before I spoke to my prophets so they could repeat what I said to them to other people. Now I mostly speak in a still small voice (1 Kin. 19:12) so that anyone who really wants to hear me will have to stop and listen, otherwise the noise of the world will drown me out. I am "the same yesterday, today and forever" (Heb. 13:9) and it is time people stop misunderstanding my plan of salvation and treating me like I am less than who I am. I was God in the flesh for a season to die for the sins of the world.

Jesus said to me, "Remember ye not the former things neither consider the things of old. Behold I will do a new thing" (Is. 43:18-19a), and shortly after that I read, "For the vision is yet for an appointed time, but at the end it shall speak, and not lie; though it tarry, wait for it; because it will surely come, it will not tarry" (Hab. 2:3).

I later read, "You shall receive power, after that the Holy Ghost is come upon you: and ye shall be witnesses unto me in Jerusalem, in Judaea, and in

Samaria, and unto the uttermost part of the earth" (Acts 1:8), letting me know that Jesus has put me in a category with some other folks with a similar message. I calmed down after reading 2 Timothy 1:7: "For God hath not given us the spirit of fear; but of power, and of love, and of a sound mind."

As far back as I can remember I have been able to write. I saw my paternal grandfather, Curtis C. Sanford, read the newspaper everyday, cover-to-cover, so I grew up thinking I needed to read something everyday myself. I think it was reading that taught me how to write. But I know writing is one of my gifts the Lord has blessed me with, and I must be obedient. Writing down my personal verses is "what thus saith the Lord" (Judg. 6:8) to me.

The Apostle Paul says, "Eye hath not seen nor ear heard, neither have entered into the hearts of [people] the things that God hath prepared for them that love him. But God hath revealed them to us by his Spirit: for the Spirit searcheth all things, yea, the deep things of God" (1 Cor. 2:9-10). Obeying God is the best expression of love for God since "to obey is better than sacrifice and to heed than the fat of rams" (1 Sam. 15:22). And because I try to be obedient, God has given me another gift that is probably the greatest of them all.

My Prayer Language, which is the gift of speaking in tongues (see 1 Cor. 12:28), is the source of the revelations I get because, sure enough, after I use my language I get a Word from the Lord. Speaking in tongues means the Spirit is doing the praying through the person's voice. So when I speak in tongues, the Holy Spirit is moving through my voice uttering his words through me that are unknown to me but that will eventually be interpreted either by me or someone else.

I have several gifts of the Spirit but I value the gift of tongues the most. John the Baptist spoke of tongues when preaching in the wilderness of Judea. He said, "I indeed baptize you with water unto repentance: but he that cometh after me is mightier than I, whose shoes I am not worthy to bear: he shall baptize you with the Holy Ghost, and with fire" (Mt. 3:11). This says to me that the blood of Jesus that was shed on the cross rather than water is what baptizes us with the

Holy Ghost—belief in the blood, that is. First John 1:7b says the blood of Jesus cleanses us from all sin. Faith in the power of the blood of Jesus to wash away sin is for me the ultimate comfort. Knowing that I do not have to worry about dying in sin and going to hell is the reason why.

Before Jesus was crucified he made a promise to his disciples saying, "I will … give you another Comforter, that he may abide with you forever: Even the Spirit of truth, whom the world cannot receive, because it seeth him not, neither knoweth him: but ye know him; for he dwelleth with you, and shall be in you" (Jn. 14:16-17).

His voice activates his Holy Spirit, meaning Jesus tells himself what to do. Later on in another chapter I will go into more detail about how the Word drives the Godhead, but right now I want to say more about the source of my revelations, which is speaking in tongues.

Jesus says in his Great Commission in the Gospel of Mark, "These signs shall follow them that believe; in my name shall they cast out devils; they shall speak with new tongues; They shall take up serpents; and if they drink any deadly thing, it shall not hurt them; they shall lay hands on the sick and they shall recover" (Mk. 16:17-18).

Some words in these verses turn off a lot of people. I am speaking of the "take up serpents" part and "if they drink any deadly thing" they will not be hurt. Jesus is talking about the devil in both cases. Back when God made man and all the beasts of the field and the fowls of the air (see Gen. 2:19) he made the serpent too. The Word says, "Now the serpent was more subtle than any beast of the field which the Lord God had made" (Gen. 3:1). As the story goes the serpent questioned Eve about what God had said about certain trees in the Garden of Eden where she and Adam were put by God to live and work. The serpent talked her into disobeying God and eating the fruit from the tree of knowledge of good and evil that was in the midst of the garden along with the tree of life (see Gen. 2:9). They could eat from every tree in the garden except the tree of knowledge of good and evil. God told Adam first and then Eve that if they ate from that tree they would surely die (see Gen. 2:15-17). Well the serpent lied to her saying, "Ye shall not surely die" (Gen. 3:4) and instead of calling on the Lord and asking him to repeat what he said Eve ate the fruit and told Adam to eat some of it. And instead of calling on the Lord and telling God about his wife's mistake and asking God what to do next, Adam ate the fruit too (see Gen. 3:5-6). So the serpent in Mark 16:18 represents the devil who is a liar. Jesus says in John 8:44 that the devil is the father of lies and that from the beginning there was no truth in him. So taking up serpents is confronting one lie after another and not believing them. And drinking any deadly thing is the enemy's attempt to destroy the believer but not being able to do so. Jesus reassures us of that when he says, "I say unto you my friends, Be not afraid of them that kill the body, and after that have no more that they can do. But I will forewarn you whom ye shall fear: Fear him, which after he hath killed hath power to cast into hell; yea, I say unto you, Fear him" (Lk. 12:4-5). And Jesus, of course, is talking about himself. Therefore, Jesus confirms that in his name there are people who will speak in tongues, of whom I am one.

Jude, the Lord's brother, says to people like me, "But ye, beloved, [build] up yourselves on your most holy faith, praying in the Holy Ghost (Jude 1:20). But perhaps the most significant aspect of tongues is that Jesus used that manifestation of his Holy Spirit to signal the start of his church. On Pentecost in Acts 2 the Word says,

> They were all with one accord in one place. And suddenly there came a sound from heaven as of a rushing mighty wind, and it filled all the house where they were sitting. And there appeared unto them cloven tongues like as of fire, and it sat upon each of them. And they were all filled with the Holy Ghost, and began to speak with other tongues, as the Spirit gave them utterance. (Acts 2:4)

Now some folks are put off by this passage because of what some denominations say about speaking in tongues, that it is the only evidence of being filled with the

Holy Spirit. I disagree because I believe there are Spirit-filled people who do not speak in tongues. However, I believe speaking in tongues is the ultimate manifestation of being Spirit-filled because it is a special gift used for sensitive divine service. Divine revelations come from speaking in tongues as well as specific divine instructions on what to do next and divine energy to obey "what thus saith the Lord," as well as divine peace for resting while waiting for the next divine assignment. And I have found from experience that people who put down speaking in tongues do not have a language themselves and are envious. But the devil has a language too just like there are false prophets, so it is not easy to tell the difference. A case in point is the devil's ability to perform miracles. Even though John the Revelator calls them lying wonders (see Rev. 13:13-14), they are miracles just the same and so is it with tongues. But the gift of tongues from God protects us from falling into traps. Jesus says in John 15:5, "For without me ye can do nothing."

Jesus also used tongues to demonstrate the inclusion of Gentiles in the gift of salvation. The Word says that Peter was preaching about Jesus, his death and resurrection, and "While Peter yet spake these words, the Holy Ghost fell on all them which heard the word. And they of the circumcision which believed were astonished, as many as came with Peter, because that on the Gentiles also was poured out the gift of the Holy Ghost. For they heard them speak with tongues, and magnify God" (Acts 10:44-46a). And that is the main reason I speak in tongues, to magnify and worship God, who, in turn, blesses me for allowing myself to be used by him in that way. I do not mind the gibberish noise or feel ashamed of sounding foolish because as the Apostle Paul says, "It pleased God by the foolishness of preaching to save them that believe" (1 Cor. 1:21).

On this subject Paul continues to say, "Forbid not to speak in tongues" (1 Cor. 14:39b) and writes, "Likewise the Spirit also helpeth our infirmities: for we know not what we should pray for as we ought: but the Spirit itself maketh intercession for us with groanings which cannot be uttered. And he that searcheth the hearts knoweth what is the mind of the Spirit, because he maketh intercession for the saints according to the will of God" (Rom. 8:26-27). Somewhat put off by "the Spirit *itself* [emphasis mine]" knowing that the Spirit is Jesus, I got all right with the passage when Paul says, "*he* maketh intercession for the saints [emphasis mine]."

Now in the Bible there are many verses with hidden meanings for me. What I mean by that is Paul makes implications about Jesus' identity in his letters. It is like he knows Jesus is God but because it is difficult for the average person to understand he hesitates to come on out and say it but instead shrouds the truth about Jesus in code. Either that was the reason or he was inhibited by the Spirit himself. Acts 16:6 says the Spirit would not let Paul preach in Asia on his third missionary journey and in 1 Corinthians 12:3 he writes that no one can say Jesus is Lord except by the Holy Ghost. Since the Bible is the Word of God written, Paul was no doubt led by the Spirit to write the way he did, and I can understand.

The best examples of Paul's writing in code for me are in the following passages. Talking about Jesus Paul says he

> is the image of the invisible God, the firstborn of every creature: For by him were all things created, that are in heaven, and that are in earth, visible and invisible, whether they be thrones, or dominions, or principalities, or powers: all things were created by him and for him: And he is before all things, and by him all things consist. And he is the head of the body, the church: who is the beginning, the first born from the dead; that in all things he might have the preeminence. For it pleased the Father that in him should all fullness dwell; and having made peace through the blood of his cross, by him to reconcile all things unto himself; by him, I say, whether they be things in earth, or things in heaven. And you, that were sometime alienated and enemies in your mind by wicked works, yet now hath he reconciled In the body of his flesh through death, to present you holy and unblamable and unreprovable in his sight. (Col. 1:15-22)

The code in this passage is verse 19, "For it pleased the Father that in him should all fullness dwell." But the hidden message to me is, "For in Jesus all fullness dwells." Verses 21 and 22 are almost straightforward about who Jesus is.

I can relate to the other example of Paul's writing in code but only up to a certain point. About Jesus he says,

> by revelation he made known unto me the mystery; (as I wrote afore in few words, Whereby, when ye read, ye may understand my knowledge in the mystery of Christ) Which in other ages was not made known unto the sons of men, as it is now revealed unto his holy apostles and prophets by the Spirit; … Whereof I was made a minister, according to the gift of the grace of God given unto me by the effectual working of his power. Unto me, who am less than the least of all saints, is this grace given, that I should preach among the Gentiles the unsearchable riches of Christ; And to make all men see what is the fellowship of the mystery, *which from the beginning of the world hath been hid in God, who created all things by Jesus Christ* [emphasis mine]: To the intent that now unto the principalities and powers in heavenly places might be known by the church the manifold wisdom of God, *According to the eternal purpose which he purposed in Christ Jesus our Lord* [emphasis mine]: In whom we have boldness and access with confidence by the faith of him. (Eph. 3:3-12)

The code in this passage is in verses 9b and 11. The hidden message to me in verse 9 is "all things were created by Jesus Christ," and verse 11 would be "According to the eternal purpose which was purposed in Christ Jesus our Lord," simple and not making a distinction in the Father and the Son since the resurrection.

Now getting back to tongues, Paul says to pray "always with all prayer and supplication in the Spirit, and [watch] thereunto with all perseverance and supplication for all saints; And for me, that utterance may be given unto me, that I

15

may open my mouth boldly, to make known the mystery of the gospel, For which I am an ambassador in bonds: that therein I may speak boldly, as I ought to speak" (Eph. 6:18-20).

Again, the gift of tongues is to magnify God (Acts 10:46), but for me, praying in the Spirit is the greatest form of prayer because years ago I was given an intercessory prayer ministry based on Matthew 10:27. There Jesus says, "What I tell you in darkness, that speak ye in light: and what ye hear in the ear, that preach ye upon the housetops." I pray for others in the Spirit and do not have to interpret my own tongues anymore because the Holy Ghost himself gives the interpretation, usually within twenty-four hours and sometimes right away. But I get filled to overflowing when praying in tongues and revelations spill out whenever I pray in the Spirit for myself or somebody else.

Jesus further told me, "You did not choose Me, but I chose you and appointed you that you should go and bear fruit, and that your fruit should remain" (Jn. 15:16), for "The Helper, the Holy Ghost ... will teach you and make you remember all that I have said. ... Let not your heart be troubled" (Jn. 14:26-27). And, "Acquaint now thyself with [Me], and be at peace: thereby good shall come unto thee" (Job 22:21). So I calmed down and accepted my assignment to share the Bible verses given to me with others.

CHAPTER 3

The Apostle Paul says, "God was manifest in the flesh" in his first letter to Timothy (3:16). Still, Paul's writing in code at other times in his epistles contributes to the resistance of seeing Jesus as the Eternal God who lived briefly as a human being. Even though Paul writes "that God was in Christ, reconciling the world unto himself" (2 Cor. 5:19), it is hard for many to accept, especially when he says at other times things like he was called to be an apostle of God "concerning his *Son* [emphasis mine] Jesus Christ our Lord" (Rom. 1:3).

Granted the incarnation made a somewhat unavoidable distinction in the Godhead for thirty some odd years and Paul's writing in code causes many people to remain stuck in preaching the Jesus who walked the earth doing good works more than preaching the Jesus that rose from the dead with all power. Forgiveness and reconciliation do not help much either since forgiveness or seeking reconciliation is a reason Christianity is difficult to practice. But the incarnation remains the real rub.

Choosing to come to earth through the seed and loins of a woman as a helpless baby instead of a full grown man who would fight and beat up the Romans offended the Jews back then who taught others to continue waiting for the Messiah. And some Christians who refuse to forgive because they see some acts as unforgivable reject Jesus who shouted forgiveness to his tormentors when hanging on the cross.

In a way the incarnation was as confusing as it was wonderful because even today over 2000 years later some people still cannot get beyond the incarnation when it comes to Jesus, insisting on keeping him subordinate to the Father in spite of the resurrection, and that is what has to stop. Jesus is now demanding that his leaders take him from flesh back to Spirit so that they can teach others to do the same but still be able to recognize him when he comes again.

Paul writes, "Christ [is] the power of God and the wisdom of God" (1 Cor. 1:24) and Isaiah expands on that definition saying Jesus is wisdom, understanding, counsel, might and knowledge (see Is. 11:2). But Jesus is beyond human comprehension, especially when it comes to his sacrificial love. Allowing himself to be captured in the Garden of Gethsemane rather than easily escaping or summoning twelve legions of angels—that is 72,000—to rescue him (see Mt. 26:53) is hard to imagine.

Jesus said to his disciples, "Greater love hath no man than this, that a man lay down his life for his friends" (Jn. 15:13). And even though Paul says, "For scarcely for a righteous man will one die: yet peradventure for a good man some would even dare to die. But God commendeth his love toward us, in that, while we were yet sinners, Christ died for us" (Rom. 8:7-8), the mystery is still there because of the wording of his explanation. That is one reason I am sharing the verses given to me: to demystify the confusing Scriptures concerning Jesus as God in spite of the incarnation that helped me see them in a different light.

The Lord says in Isaiah 46:9-10, "Remember the former things of old: for I am God, and there is none else; I am God and there is none like me, Declaring the end from the beginning, and from ancient times the things that are not yet done, saying, My counsel shall stand, and I will do all my pleasure."

What we sometimes fail to see is God is sovereign and does what he wants saying, "Look unto me, and be saved, all the ends of the earth: for I am God, and there is none else" (Is. 45:22). God thought up the plan of salvation and carried it out his way, whether we like it or not.

CHAPTER 4

"For there are three that bear record in heaven, the Father, the Word, and the Holy Ghost: and these three are one" (1 Jn. 5:7). A phrase that explains the Trinity in an understandable way is "thought, Word, and deed." Thought is God the Father supported in Isaiah 14:24. It says, "The Lord of hosts hath sworn, saying, Surely as I have thought, so shall it come to pass; and as I have purposed, so shall it stand." Word is God the Son in John 1:1-3 and 14, which say, "In the beginning was the Word, and the Word was with God, and the Word was God. The same was in the beginning with God. All things were made by him; and without him was not any thing made that was made. And the Word was made flesh, and dwelt among us ... full of grace and truth." And, deed is God the Holy Spirit, the activity or movement of God in Genesis 1:1-2: "In the beginning God created the heaven and the earth. And the earth was without form, and void; and darkness was upon the face of the deep. And the Spirit of God *moved* upon the face of the waters" [emphasis mine].

Paul almost refers to thought, Word, and deed in this verse: "Whatsoever ye do in word or deed, do all in the name of the Lord Jesus, giving thanks to God and the Father by him" (Col. 3:17). So now I will provide support for my thought, Word, and deed verses given to me.

In the Trinity, God the Father is original thought. The revelation I received is that before creation God was thinking. But it is only after creation that anything, including Scripture, can speak of God's thinking, which it does through the prophets and others in the Old Testament and Jesus himself in the New Testament. For example, "The word which came to Jeremiah from the Lord" says, "If that nation, against whom I have pronounced, turn from their evil, I will repent of the evil that I thought to do unto them" (Jer. 18:8).

Another Old Testament prophet says, "For, lo, he that formeth the mountains, and createth the wind, and declareth unto man what is his thought, that maketh the morning darkness, and treadeth upon the high places of the earth, The Lord, The God of hosts, is his name" (Amos 4:13).

The word of the Lord came to Zechariah saying, "Thus saith the Lord of hosts" (Zech. 1:3), "My words and my statutes which I commanded my servants the prophets, did they not [say] ... Like as the Lord of hosts thought to do unto us, according to our ways, and according to our doings, so hath he dealt with us" (Zech. 1:6).

"For thus saith the Lord of hosts; As I thought to punish you, when your fathers provoked me to wrath, saith the Lord of hosts, and I repented not: so again have I thought in these days to do well unto Jerusalem and to the house of Judah" (Zech. 8:14-15a).

The Psalmist David says, "Many, O Lord my God, are thy wonderful works which thou hast done, and thy thoughts which are to us-ward: they cannot be reckoned up in order unto thee: if I would declare and speak of them, they are more than can be numbered" (Ps. 40:5).

"How precious also are thy thoughts unto me, O God! How great is the sum of them!" (Ps. 139:17).

Another Psalmist says, "O Lord, how great are thy works! And thy thoughts are very deep" (Ps. 92:5).

And Isaiah the prophet whose words were given to me first supporting God the Father as thought goes on to say, "For my thoughts are not your thoughts, neither are your ways my ways, saith the Lord. For as the heavens are higher than the earth, so are my ways higher than your ways, and my thoughts than your thoughts" (Is. 55:8-9).

Finally, the prophet Jeremiah writes of the thoughts of God while at the same time confirming my need to be faithful to my assignment. He says, "For I know the thoughts that I think toward you, saith the Lord, thoughts of peace, and not of evil, to give you an expected end" (Jer. 29:11). But the main thing the prophet says for my benefit is, "The anger of the Lord shall not return, until he

[has] executed and till he [has] performed the thoughts of his heart: in the later days ye shall consider it perfectly" (Jer. 23:20).

In the Trinity, God the Son is Word. It was revealed to me that the Word drives the Godhead. By that I mean, the Father hears the Word and the Spirit hears the Word and responds.

For example, when Jesus was at the tomb of Lazarus and told the men with Martha to take the stone away, after they did, "Jesus lifted up his eyes and said, Father, I thank thee that thou hast *heard* me [emphasis mine]. And I knew that thou *hearest* me always" [emphasis mine] (Jn. 11:41-42).

About the Spirit Jesus says, "When he, the Spirit of truth, is come, he will guide you into all truth: for he shall not speak of himself; but whatsoever he shall *hear* [emphasis mine] that shall he speak: and he will shew you things to come" (Jn. 16:13), which means emphasis is placed on the spoken word in Scripture and in life.

People cannot read minds. It is when someone speaks that others can learn what is on that person's mind if he or she is telling the truth. The same is so with God, which is why the spoken word has power.

Jesus is the articulation of divine thought, begotten when God's thoughts were sounded by the Holy Spirit in words that "call[ed] those things which be not as though they were" (Rom. 4:17).

For example, at creation "God said, Let there be light"(Gen. 1:3); "Let there be a firmament in the midst of the waters" (Gen. 1:6); "Let the waters under the heaven be gathered together" (Gen. 1:9); "Let the earth bring forth grass" (Gen. 1:11); "Let there be lights in the firmament" (Gen. 1:14); "Let the waters bring forth … life" (Gen. 1:20); and, "Let the earth bring forth the living creature" (Gen. 1:24).

But the main creation verse for me is, "Let *us* [emphasis mine] make man in our image, after our likeness" (Gen. 1:26), indicating that the Trinity has always been. The Godhead has always been active thinking, speaking, and acting.

21

Before creation God talked to himself. After creation God continued to talk to himself during the incarnation when he prayed. God has always spoken to humans from Adam and Eve, to Cain, to Noah, to Abraham, Isaac, and Jacob, to the prophets, to Mary and his earthly family, to John the Baptist, to the disciples, the apostles, to other people today and to me.

I believe that means when Jesus speaks we are hearing from eternity just like the hymn "Lift Him Up" says—that I learned when I was a girl and still sing today, especially at Annual Conference in the African Methodist Episcopal Church. Emphasis is placed on the spoken word in Scripture to teach about God.

Jesus said to the devil who tempted him forty days in the wilderness, "It is written ... Thou shalt not tempt the Lord thy God" (Mt. 4:7). The devil was tempting him and Jesus was referring to what was written about himself.

Jesus said to the centurion in Capernaum whose servant was sick, "I will come and heal him" (Mt. 8:10). He did not say he would pray for the power to heal or get permission to perform any miracle.

Jesus said to Caiaphas the high priest after he asked him if he were the Christ, "I am" (Mk. 14:62a). But for me his greatest words were spoken on Calvary.

Jesus said while hanging on the cross, "Father, forgive them for they know not what they do" (Lk. 23:43), talking out loud to his thoughts in heaven. To the thief on the cross next to him he said, "Verily I say unto thee, today shalt thou be with me in paradise" (Lk. 23:43). To Mary he said, "Woman, behold thy son." To John his disciple he said, "Behold thy mother" (Jn. 19:25-27). Jesus was talking to himself again when he said, "Eloi, eloi, lama sabach-thani?" which means, "My God, my God, why hast thou forsaken me?" (Mk. 15:33-34) as if to say, "What have I done to myself?" To the Roman executioners he said, "I thirst" (Jn. 19:28). Finally, to himself again he said, "It is finished" (Jn. 19:30) and "Father, into thy hands I commend my spirit" (Lk. 23:46) or "I am reuniting with all of myself."

Jesus said to his disciples after he rose from the dead, "All power is given unto me in heaven and in earth" (Mt. 28:18), declaring the power of the resurrection.

Jesus said to Mary Magdalene and the other Mary (probably his mother) after he rose from the dead, "Go tell my brethren to go into Galilee and there shall they see me" (Mt. 28:10).

Jesus said to Saul whom he struck down on the road to Damascus who was on his way to persecute Christians, "It is hard for thee to kick against the pricks. ... I am Jesus whom thou persecutest" (Acts 26:14-15). Paul was hurting himself more than the Christians he oppressed, which just goes to show he had to learn about Jesus like everybody else.

In the Trinity, God the Holy Spirit is deed. The Spirit does what he hears himself say, so evidence that the Word drives the Godhead in the activity or movement of God is the most prominent when focusing not on what the Holy Spirit does but on what the Spirit says.

For example, the Spirit comes upon the prophets enabling them to speak what "thus saith the Lord" (Jer. 22:30). The prophet Ezekiel said, "The hand of the Lord was upon me, and carried me out in the spirit of the Lord" (Ez. 37:1).

The Lord said to Ezekiel, "And ye shall know that I am the Lord, when ... [I] shall put my spirit in you, and ye shall live" (Ez. 37:13-14).

Jesus said to his disciples, "And ye shall be brought before governors and kings for my sake, for a testimony against them and the Gentiles. But when they deliver you up, take no thought how or what ye shall speak: for it shall be given you in that same hour what ye shall speak. For it is not ye that speak but the Spirit of your Father which speaketh in you" (Mt. 10:18-20). Jesus is talking about himself because he is called The everlasting Father in Isaiah 9:6.

Jesus said to some Pharisees who were arguing with him, "If I cast out devils by the Spirit of God, then the kingdom of God is come unto you" (Mk. 8:12).

Jesus "sighed deeply in his spirit" (Mk. 8:12) when questioning some Pharisees about seeking a sign from heaven to prove his identity.

"And Jesus being full of the Holy Ghost returned from Jordan, and was led by the Spirit into the wilderness, Being forty days tempted of the devil. And in those days he did eat nothing" (Lk. 4:1-2a). It is the Spirit that fills and sustains when a body goes without food that long.

The New Millennial Covenant interpretation of "the Spirit said" verses is that Jesus talked to himself in his thoughts and out loud telling himself what to do from doing good, to confronting the devil, to going to the cross.

For example, after Jesus was tempted by the devil he "returned in the power of the Spirit into Galilee" (Lk. 4:14) again telling himself what to do and doing it.

> And [Jesus] came to Nazareth, where he had been brought up: and, as his custom was, he went into the synagogue on the Sabbath day, and stood up for to read. And there was delivered unto him the book of the prophet Isaiah. And when he had opened the book, he found the place where it was written, The Spirit of the Lord is upon me, because he hath anointed me to preach the gospel to the poor; he hath sent me to heal the brokenhearted, to preach deliverance to the captives, and recovering of sight to the blind, to set at liberty them that are bruised, To preach the acceptable year of the Lord. And he closed the book, and he gave it again to the minister and sat down. And the eyes of all them that were in the synagogue were fastened on him. And he began to say unto them, This day is this Scripture fulfilled in your ears. (Lk. 4:16-21)

For me, this passage—more than any other Scripture—speaks of Jesus and the Spirit as one.

In teaching his disciples how to pray, Jesus said, "If ye then, being evil, know how to give good gifts unto your children: how much more shall your heavenly Father give the Holy Spirit to them that ask him?" (Lk. 11:1-3). Jesus was talking about himself prior to the incarnation and after the resurrection.

Jesus said to the Pharisee named Nicodemus, "Verily, verily I say unto thee, Except a man be born of water and of the Spirit, he cannot enter into the kingdom of God. That which is born of the flesh is flesh; and that which is born of the Spirit is spirit" (Jn. 3:5-6). Here Jesus is talking about his temporary duality during the incarnation. He is both flesh and blood and spirit. His body that he got from Mary is flesh but his mind that generates supernatural activity when he thinks, speaks and acts is pure spirit.

"The wind bloweth where it listeth, and thou hearest the sound thereof, but canst not tell whence it cometh, and whither it goeth: so is every one that is born of the spirit" (Jn 3:8). To me this is saying that human beings are created in the image of God and are capable of supernatural activity too although with vast limitations.

Spirit-filled individuals see with more than just their eyes, hear with more than just their ears, and feel with more than just their emotions.

Jesus said to a Samaritan woman, "The hour cometh, and now is, when the true worshipers shall worship the Father in spirit and in truth: for the Father seeketh such to worship him. God is *a* Spirit [emphasis mine] and they that worship him must worship him in spirit and in truth" (Jn. 4:23-24). Verse 23 is a continuation of John 14:6 where Jesus says, "I am the way, the truth and the life: no [one] cometh unto the Father, but by me," which is a continuation of "He that hath seen me hath seen the Father" (Jn. 14:9) and "The Father and I are one" (Jn. 10:30).

But verse 24 more than any other verse shows me how the Spirit is Jesus' movement and activity because he says, "God is a Spirit," not some spirits, not a few spirits, not many spirits, but a Spirit that is true, Jesus being made a Spirit again by "the power of his resurrection" (Phil. 3:10).

Jesus says to the disciples that did not desert him, "It is the spirit that quickeneth; the flesh profiteth nothing" (Jn. 6:63). Quickeneth means make alive.

25

A verse that explains quickeneth is Job 27:3 that says, "The spirit of God is in my nostrils," meaning one's breath. Jesus goes on to say in that same verse, "the words that I speak unto you, they are spirit, and they are life." Jesus is the Word made flesh speaking spiritually about abundant life in him (see Jn. 10:10).

"Then the Spirit said unto Philip, Go near, and join thyself to this chariot" (Acts 8:29), where the Ethiopian eunuch was in order to explain what he was reading from the prophet Isaiah (see Acts 8:26-39).

Peter had a vision one time when he was hungry about heaven and a sheet that came down with all kinds of birds, animals and creeping things on it. He heard a voice say, "Rise, Peter; kill, and eat" (Acts 10:13) but protested saying he did not eat anything common or unclean. The voice spoke again saying, "What God hath cleansed, that call not thou common" (Acts 10:15). And, "While Peter thought on the vision, the Spirit said unto him, Behold, three men seek thee" (Acts 10:19). That is similar to what happened to me when the Lord told me to write down and share the Bible verses given to me; I protested but Jesus won the argument.

CHAPTER 5

People seem to be able to understand the concept of God the Father and God the Son, which contributes to separating the Godhead more into two persons than three mainly because of the difficulty in conceptualizing the Holy Spirit. That is why "thought, Word and deed" is helpful, deed being the activity or movement of God. It is easy to see that since we human beings can think, speak and act the phrase shows how we are created in the image of God, the original thought, Word and deed.

The Holy Spirit is the mind, breath, and invisible body of God prior to the incarnation and after the resurrection, Jesus having been "all the fullness of the Godhead bodily" (Col. 2:9) when he walked the earth. Since the Holy Spirit has always done the work of the Godhead including *sounding* the Word at creation, calling "those things which be not as though they were" (Rom. 4:17), the Bible focuses on the supernatural. Why, because the Holy Spirit sounds the Word and obeys himself. The Spirit acted and "formed man from the dust of the ground and breathed into his nostrils the breath of life and man became a living soul" (Gen. 2:7). Then the Spirit's voice called Adam in the Garden of Eden and asked him and Eve what they had done when they had eaten the forbidden fruit (see Gen. 2:9-13). The Spirit's voice called Cain asking him about his brother Abel whom he had slain because he was jealous of him (Gen. 4:9). He called Noah to build the ark before bringing the floodwaters to destroy the world and start over (see Gen. 6:14-22). He called Abram from his father's house and told him to go to a land that he would show him (Gen. 12:1), made a covenant with him to be his God and changed his name to Abraham and his wife Sarai to Sarah (see Gen. 17:1-16). Making himself an angel he called Abraham and told him to stay his hand and not kill his son Isaac (see Gen. 22:1-13). He called Rebekah, Isaac's wife, and told her that two nations were in her womb and that the older would serve the younger (Gen. 25:23). The Spirit's voice told Jacob to go to Bethel then changed Jacob's name to Israel (Gen. 35:10). His voice called Moses from a burning bush that was not consumed (Ex. 3:2) and told him to go tell Pharaoh King of Egypt to let his people go (Ex. 3:10). His voice called Joshua, the son of Nun, and told him, "As I was with Moses, so I will be with you" (Josh. 1:5). His voice called the prophets by name and told them to tell others what "thus saith the Lord" (Ex. 4:22) or, to put it another way, what he said to them. Samuel was called when a mere child (see 1 Sam. 3:1-21). He called Elijah the Tishbite (1 Kin. 17:1) and fed him by ravens (1 Kin. 17:4). He called Elisha and let him make an ax head float (see 2 Kin. 6:1-7). He asked Job, "Where were you when I laid the foundations of the earth" (Job 38:4) and "when the morning stars sang together" (Job 38:7). He called David to sing (Ps. 8:1) and play the harp (1 Sam. 16:23) for him. He spoke to Solomon twice, in Gibeon and when the temple was built and dedicated (see 1 Kin. 9:1-9) to show his support. He called Isaiah the son of Amoz in the year that King Uzziah died asking, "Whom shall I send and who will go for Us? [meaning thought, Word and deed] Then [Isaiah] said, "Here am I! Send me" (Is. 6:8). He said to Jeremiah, "Before I formed you in the womb I knew you" (Jer. 1:5). He asked Ezekiel in a vision about a valley, "Can these dry bones live?" (Eze. 37:3). He told Hosea to marry and care for a whore (Hos. 1:2). He made himself an angel another time and told Joseph not to be afraid to take Mary as his wife because, "that which is conceived in her is of the Holy Ghost" (Mt. 1:20), talking about the way he chose to come into the world. He had the angel Gabriel tell Mary, "The Holy Ghost shall come upon thee, and the power of the Highest shall overshadow thee: therefore also that holy thing which shall be born of thee shall be called the Son of God" (Lk. 1:35), meaning he would conceive himself through his own power, describe himself in supernatural terms and give himself the everlasting name of Savior. He called to his cousin John in his mother Elizabeth's womb when he himself was in Mary's womb causing John to leap for joy (see Lk. 1:39-45). And, of course, he called his twelve disciples by name during his incarnation and has been calling disciples ever since. But the main supernatural call the Spirit sounded was himself from the dead out of the tomb. The Spirit's human voice said, "I lay down my life, that

28

I might take it again. No man taketh it from me, but I lay it down of myself. I have power to lay it down, and I have power to take it again. This commandment have I received of my Father" (Jn. 10:17b-18). The hidden meaning of verse 18b would be, "This commandment have I received of myself." And the Spirit's voice teaches and guides us today giving some of us divine revelations to see the Spirit personified in Jesus with a mind, a voice and a body.

The prophet Jeremiah speaking for God says, "Behold, I will ... reveal unto them the abundance of peace and truth" (Jer. 33:6). "And all thy children shall be taught of the Lord; and great shall be the peace of thy children" (Is. 54:13), although that depends on the revelation because the assignment to write down and share the Bible verses given to me was anything but peaceful. A case in point is the verse that says, "Take heed therefore unto yourselves, and to all the flock, over the which the Holy Ghost hath made you overseers to feed the church of God, which he hath purchased with his own blood" (Acts 20:28). I felt like Moses, totally inadequate (Ex. 3:11), like Jeremiah, naïve and unworthy (Jer. 1:6), and like Ezekiel saying, "O Lord, I don't know" (Eze. 37:3). Paul refers to Jesus as God and head of his church. The burden is therefore put on preachers today to feed the church fresh spiritual food, the old messages being leftovers. Comfort for me came from Jeremiah 29:11: "I know the plans I have for you, says the Lord, plans to prosper you and not to harm you; plans to give you a future and a hope."

The Holy Spirit's role in prayer further complicates people's ability to see him as Jesus. For example, praying in the Spirit—also known as using a prayer language—is over the top for some Christians because nowhere in the Bible does it say Jesus used a language although I believe John 11:33 says he did. "Jesus groaned in the Spirit and was troubled" before raising Lazarus from the dead. This makes me believe he spoke in tongues for in this kind of prayer, "The Spirit pleads with God in groans too deep for words" (Rom. 8:26). To me that sounds like God is speaking to himself in spiritual words he alone understands. And I believe anytime Jesus prayed to the Father he was speaking his own thoughts out loud.

The Holy Spirit is the source of grace. "The anointing which you have received from him abides in you. As long as his Spirit remains in you, you do not need anyone to teach you. For his Spirit teaches you about everything, and what he teaches is true, not false. Obey the Spirit's teaching, then, and remain in union with Christ" (1 Jn. 2:27).

This verse applies to me and has to do with the various gifts people have. There are writers, educators, speakers, singers, dancers, athletes, scientists, engineers, technicians, and so on. The list is endless because I believe everybody born into the world has at least one gift and no one is "giftless." That means everyone is a recipient of grace whether he or she believes in God or not. Why, because life itself is a gift.

Genesis 1:27 says, "God created man in his own image, in the image of God created he him; male and female created he them." Our ability to breathe is a manifestation of the Spirit of God in us. And being able to do anything is the movement of the Holy Spirit also known as grace.

Since the Holy Spirit manifests himself in our minds, bodies and spirits, the Apostle Paul found it necessary to say, "Walk not after the flesh but after the Spirit" (Rom. 8:1) for "where sin abounded, grace did much more abound: That as sin hath reigned unto death, even so might grace reign through righteousness unto eternal life by Jesus Christ our Lord" (Rom. 5:20b-21). We all sin and we all have a certain amount of grace even though not all of us are willing to concede that the Holy Spirit is the source of grace or that we were born in sin. But the reality of death becomes apparent eventually. According to James 1:15 sin is the origin of death. David says in Psalm 51:5, "Behold, I was shapen in iniquity; and in sin did my mother conceive me." So since even newborn babies die, original sin must be the cause.

That is why perhaps the greatest manifestation of grace occurred when Jesus was nailed to the cross, expressed later in his words to Paul: "My grace is

30

sufficient for thee: for my strength is made perfect in weakness" (2 Cor. 12:9).
This reveals his mindset when hanging on the cross. Jesus knew he was suffering
out of love for his creation. He knew his flesh was dying for the sins of the world.
He knew his blood was being shed to wash away sin, something only the blood of
God can do. So in his weakest moment things could not have been more perfect
because he was accomplishing his purpose for coming into the world.

> For the law of the Spirit of life in Christ Jesus hath made [us] free
> from the law of sin and death. For what the law could not do, in
> that it was weak through the flesh, God sending his own Son in the
> likeness of sinful flesh, and for sin, condemned sin in the flesh.
> (Rom. 8:2-3)

The hidden meaning of verse 3 is "For what the law could not do, in that it was
weak through the flesh, [God's coming to earth in the likeness of sinful flesh for
sin] condemned sin in the flesh."

The Bible speaks of Peter's hearing directly from the Holy Ghost in verses
like Acts 10:19: "While Peter thought on the vision, the Spirit said unto him,
Behold, three men seek thee," and Acts 11:12, "The Spirit bade me go with them,
nothing doubting." The Holy Ghost speaks giving instructions and directions to
those he chooses. He also comforts, which to me is his best work.

I say that because there are times when nothing but comfort will do. We
can have health, money, material things, and success. But because there is death
or even the threat of death, we need comfort more than anything else. For me,
comfort translates into "the peace that passeth all understanding" (Phil. 4:7).

Death represents loss, the loss of life being the ultimate loss. But there is
loss of health, employment, finances, property, lifestyle from acts of nature like
fires, floods, hurricanes, tornados, earthquakes, drought, heat, and cold; loss of
wellbeing from humiliation, betrayal, guilt, deception, rejection, fear. There is the
loss of love, companionship, friendship all forms of death: the death of a
marriage, relationships, and peace of mind. The list goes on and on. That is why
the Holy Spirit's role as Comforter is the most needed for me.

Before he was crucified, Jesus said to his disciples, "It is expedient for you that I go away: for if I go not away, the Comforter will not come unto you; but if I depart, I will send him unto you" (Jn. 16:7). In this verse Jesus is talking about his resurrected Holy Spirit, because his death and resurrection is the origin of the Holy Spirit as Comforter. He goes on to say in the passage why the Comforter is so important saying when he comes

> he will reprove the world of sin, and of righteousness, and of judgment: Of sin, because they believe not on me; of righteousness, because I go to my Father, and ye see me no more; Of judgment, because the prince of this world is judged. I have yet many things to say unto you, but ye cannot bear them now. (Jn. 16:8-12)

But it is verse 10 that stands out to me. Here Jesus says, "Of righteousness, because I go to my Father, and ye see me no more." Jesus says in John 4:24, "God is *a* Spirit [emphasis mine]: and they that worship him must worship him in spirit and in truth." So if God is a Spirit and he is going back to his Father who is a spirit and not a person like he is, Jesus is saying after the resurrection he will go back to being pure spirit again, his Holy Spirit doing the work of reuniting his flesh with his original thoughts. And verse 12 is significant for me because Jesus was telling his disciples that he has many more things to say to them but that they are not ready to hear. But in times like these, perhaps believers are ready now.

CHAPTER 6

Jesus is the only person of the Godhead as a result of the incarnation, which put him on the defensive as a twelve year old with his parents when they found him in the temple talking with the scholars (see Lk. 2:49) and during his entire ministry. This is due in part to his sovereignty as God and his obvious decision not to act as expected in human terms.

I mean, what kind of God would condescend to leave his lofty throne on high to come down here as a human being and have to do all that humans have to do just to earn a living and survive, not to mention having to suffer and glimpse death when others die then eventually eyeball death himself and give up the ghost. That does not make a lot of sense and yet that is pretty much what God did when he put on flesh and came to earth.

The gospel of Luke records Jesus' birth saying that in those days Caesar Augustus sent out a decree that the people in his empire should be taxed. So Joseph went from Nazareth in Galilee to Bethlehem in Judea with his pregnant wife, Mary, to be registered. There was no room for them in the inn when they got to town and had to stay in a stable. Mary gave birth to Jesus amongst the cattle, wrapped him in strips of cloth and laid him in a manger.

Now again the human question would be what real God would allow himself to be born amongst piles of manure and be put in a trough with animals breathing on him. No matter the angel with the shepherds or the heavenly host singing (see Lk. 2:8-14) or the star in the east that led the three wise men to where he was or the gifts they gave him (see Mt. 2:1-11). He was still a helpless baby who had to be fed and changed and taken care of in every way. Now seriously, what kind of real God would do such a thing to himself?

He had that run-in with his family as a pre-teen that time in Jerusalem at Passover when he supposedly got lost. When found in the temple talking with the priests, implied in the passage is that when they left he was yelled at and put on some kind of punishment (see Lk. 2:49-51). Luke says, "When they saw him, they were amazed: and his mother said unto him, Son, why hast thou thus dealt with us? behold, thy father and I have sought thee sorrowing" (Lk. 2:48). "And he went down with them, and came to Nazareth, and was subject unto them" (Lk. 2:51). Now honestly, what kind of real God would have to do something like leave the supper table and go to bed without dessert? Yet the Word says Jesus had parents who raised him and a mother who told him what to do even when he was grown.

Take the wedding at Cana for instance. It was his mother Mary who told Jesus the couple had no wine to serve their guests. Jesus told her in so many words it was not his problem, but evidently she convinced him to the contrary because she told the servants to do whatever he said and he ended up turning big waterpots filled with water into fine white wine (see Jn. 2:1-11). Now seriously, what kind of real God would listen to a woman in that day and time, mother or not?

Jesus "went about doing good, and healing" (Acts 10:38) but he spent an inordinate amount of time defending himself, as far as I am concerned. Take John the Baptist, his forerunner, for instance. He recognized Jesus by his walk one day saying "Behold the lamb of God, which taketh away the sin of the world" (Jn. 1:29).

John baptized Jesus (see Mt. 3:13-17) and saw the Spirit descending and resting on him like a dove (Jn. 1:32). But then later he sent word asking Jesus if he were the Messiah or should they look for another (Lk. 7:19). "Jesus answering said unto them, 'Go your way, and tell John what things ye have seen and heard; how the blind see, the lame walk, the lepers are cleansed, the deaf hear, the dead are raised, to the poor the gospel is preached. And blessed is he, whosoever shall not be offended in me'" (Lk. 7:22-23). I believe John lost his head for doing that and that Herodias was just the instrument used (see Mt. 14:6-11).

Jesus fed thousands of folks (see Mt. 14:19-21) and they followed him but he complained that they did so not to hear his words but to get more food (see Jn. 6:26). He even had to defend himself with his own disciples. Responding to

34

Thomas who doubted and played dumb sometimes Jesus said, "If ye had known me, ye should have known my Father also: and from henceforth ye know him, and have seen him" (Jn. 14:7). To Philip he said, "Have I been so long time with you, and yet hast thou not known me, Philip? He that hath seen me hath seen the Father; and how sayest thou then, Shew us the Father?" (Jn. 14:9). To some argumentative Jews he said, "The Father and I are one" (Jn. 10:30) and they took up rocks to stone him (see Jn. 14:31). In these verses Jesus is being straightforward about who he is.

It helps that Paul writes, "God was manifest in the flesh" in a letter to Timothy (1 Tim. 3:16) and "In [Jesus] dwelleth all the fullness of the Godhead bodily" to the church at Colosse (Col. 2:9). His saying, "We speak before God in Christ" (2 Cor. 12:19) to the Corinthian church is also helpful. Still nothing takes away from the fact that the incarnation put Jesus at a disadvantage in more ways than one, especially when it comes to taking Jesus from flesh back to Spirit. Even though the Father calls the Son God in Hebrews 1:8 and Paul says, "God ... created all things by Jesus Christ" in Ephesians 3:9, the incarnation interferes with "men see[ing] what is the fellowship of the mystery." Even though, "All things were created by him and for him" (Col. 1:16) the cliché, "Familiarity breeds contempt," applies because it is hard to believe God would want to go to the trouble of having to eliminate waste, wash his hands, wait in line, and pay taxes.

So I shall now write an explanation of Jesus and who he is based on the Bible verses given to me.

The word "Trinity," which means three, is not in the Bible. But when Jesus says in Matthew 28:19, "Go ye therefore and teach all nations, baptizing them in the name of the Father, and of the Son, and of the Holy Ghost," the term Trinity emerges. And that word is the cause of much confusion.

But, it was revealed to me that back before time God lived in darkness and swirling water mulling things over in his mind, talking to himself in silence about his future plans. We read in 1 Kings 8:12 that "The Lord said he would dwell in thick darkness." God thought about and discussed with himself how he would

35

create the universe and, in particular, a world where he could participate in daily life.

The beginning of the Old Testament reads, "In the beginning God created the heaven and the earth. And the earth was without form, and void; and darkness was upon the face of the deep. And the Spirit of God moved upon the face of the waters" (Gen. 1:1-2). The amount of time God spent thinking is, of course, unknown, especially since "one day is with the Lord as a thousand years, and a thousand years as one day" (2 Pet. 3:8). No one knows how long God was in darkness either and we have no way of knowing. What can be inferred from Scripture is that God made the decision to speak and create the world.

The first words God said were, "Let there be light" according to Genesis 1:3, again, calling himself into visibility as the light of the world four days before he made the sun. Darkness did not go anywhere; light was just added. Then reading on in Genesis 1 we see that God spoke more words and created other things.

He separated light from darkness and called them day and night. He made a firmament, which is space, to divide the waters. He called the firmament heaven and evidently there is water over heaven like there is water below the firmament because Genesis 1:7 says the firmament divides them.

We read that God told the waters on earth to gather together so we have oceans, seas, rivers, lakes, streams, creeks, ponds, wells, waterfalls, and so on. After that he told dry land to appear.

If we keep on reading Genesis 1 we see that God spoke everything into existence: grass, trees, fruit; the sun and other stars, the moon and all the planets, birds, fish, animals, insects, worms and other creeping things, cattle and beasts like dinosaurs and elephants. God created everything.

Then God made man, meaning humankind, in his own image. That means even though God is spirit he still has a face and a body with hands because he "formed" us from the dust of the ground and our breath is what makes us living souls (see Gen. 2:7). And in Exodus 33:20 God told Moses no one could see his face and live. So even though God is spirit (see Jn 4:24) and has a spiritual body, for thirty-three or so years he walked the earth in a flesh and blood body.

Now Genesis 1:26 is where the Trinity comes in. It was there all along but it was not spoken about until verse 26. It says, "Let us make man in our image after our likeness." The "us" is God the Father, God the Son, and God the Holy Ghost in the person of Jesus. Jesus is the only person of the Godhead and the only part of God human beings can claim to know, because he condescended to become like us for a season.

People like Moses and the prophets heard God's voice, which was Jesus. John 1:1-3 and 14 say, "In the beginning was the Word and the Word was with God and the Word was God. The same was in the beginning with God. All things were made by him and without him was not anything made that was made. And the Word was made flesh and dwelt among us … full of grace and truth." Jesus is the Word.

We Christians have been taught certain things about Jesus like he was called the Son of God and the Son of Man. He had a mother named Mary and sisters and brothers. Two of his brothers were named James and Jude who wrote books in the New Testament, and two others were named Simon and Joseph (see Mt. 13:55).

The Scripture tells us that Jesus walked the earth and "went about doing good" (Acts 10:38). He healed the sick (Mt. 8:14-17), opened the ears of the deaf (Mk. 7:31-37), gave sight to the blind (Mk. 10:46-52), fed the hungry (Jn. 6:1-15), cast out demons (Lk. 8:26-39) and walked on water (Mk. 6:45-51). He even raised the dead (Lk. 7:11-17). He wept (Jn. 11:35) and he prayed, calling God "Father" (see Mt. 6:9). Yet Jesus says in John 10:30, "The Father and I are one." That goes back to Genesis 1:26: "Let us make man in our image." That verse is saying that Jesus was talking to himself.

A phrase to better understand the term Trinity is thought, Word, and deed. Thought is God the Father supported in Isaiah 14:24. It says, "Surely as I have thought, so shall it come to pass; and as I have purposed, so shall it stand." Word is God the Son, again in John 1:1-3 and 14. And deed is God the Holy Ghost, again the activity or movement of God in Genesis 1:1-2.

Thoughts are words so Jesus, the Word, was before the foundation of the world (see Jn. 17:24). But when God thought to utter sound and did, that is the moment Jesus was begotten. Jesus is the voice of God (see Ps. 29), the words spoken, the articulation of divine thought. God's thoughts are wisdom, understanding, counsel, might and knowledge (see Is. 11:2), among other things I am incapable of comprehending.

Now as soon as God opened God's mouth and spoke, what God said happened; for example, when God said, "Let there be light" (Gen. 1:3) there it was. When God said, "Let dry land appear" (Gen. 1:9) there it was. As soon as God said it, it happened. So, when God spoke and things happened that was the work of the Holy Ghost. It is through the Holy Spirit that God called "those things which be not as though they were" (Rom. 4:17). And it is the Holy Spirit that "sounds" the Word.

All this activity occurred at the same time. That is, all three things happened at once. God thought, God spoke, and every time God said something, it happened. That is how God is three in one. So the familiar phrase thought, Word, and deed can help us remember. Methodists say the phrase "thought, word and deed" in the Holy Communion litany.

So the Trinity is one God who does three major things always and at the same time: he thinks, speaks and acts. That is how human beings are created in the image of God: we too can think, speak, and act, but with vast limitations, of course.

From Scripture I inferred that thousands of years after the world was created, God made another decision and that was for the flesh part of himself to come down from heaven and walk the earth. That is called the incarnation, God in the flesh.

So God as thought who decided to speak became a man, born of a woman, which means the Word was made flesh. God's original thoughts and Holy Spirit

38

as Comforter remained in heaven, which is why Jesus prayed to the Father when he was on earth. He was really talking to himself but in order not to overload people's circuits, he called that part of his mind Father. Implied in this is the idea that only some of his thoughts were with him on earth—only what a human brain could handle; his other thoughts remained in heaven.

Jesus grew up and learned the carpentry trade from his stepfather Joseph. He lived about thirty-three years. His ministry lasted about three years before he was killed. He was crucified, died and was buried. However, it is after he rose from the dead that I learned of another divine decision.

Jesus says in Matthew 28:18 that he has all power in heaven and in earth. He means all power everywhere. This indicates that God the Father—original thought—deferred to his spoken word after the resurrection. To put it another way, defer means to yield. God respectfully yielded his thoughts to what he said after he rose from the dead. So emphasis now should be placed on Jesus who is the physical manifestation of divine thought and activity. Jesus is the same as the Father and the Holy Ghost from before the foundation of the world and especially after his resurrection and ascension, having shed his flesh.

Referring to himself, Jesus says in John 15:26, "When the Comforter comes, whom I will send to you from the Father, even the Spirit of truth who proceeds from the Father, He will testify of me." This is yet another verse that talks about how God dialogues with himself.

God can do that because God is sovereign. God defines God's Self. God does what God wants to do and when. Colossians 2:9 says Jesus is "all the fullness of the Godhead bodily."

Finally, when I read verses that say Jesus sits at the right hand of the Father, I learned in seminary that that is root power, not a physical place. Revelation 7:17 says Jesus is in the midst of the throne and there is only one throne even though speaking to his disciples Jesus says in Matthew 19:28, "Ye which have followed me, in the regeneration when the Son of man shall sit in the throne of his glory, ye also shall sit upon twelve thrones, judging the twelve tribes of Israel."

So the Trinity is not three persons. There is one God and his name is Jesus. And when Christ comes again his name will change from Jesus to The Word of God according to Revelation 19:13.

The various names of God are expressions of what he is doing at the time. For example, Jehovah Rapha is the healer, Jehovah Shalom is the peacemaker, Jehovah Raah is the shepherd (Marshall 15), and so on. We know of other names for God in the Old Testament such as Elohim (Gen. 1:1) and El Shaddai (Gen. 35:11). In seminary I was taught the names Yahweh and Adoni. But Jesus is the only name I need to know. Why, because Jesus means Savior. If I believe in Jesus I will not die and go to hell but live with him forever in heaven. And there is power in the name Jesus. This power enables me to move in the gifts of the Spirit for greater service. This power is what makes people able to prophesy and work miracles. Believers can heal the sick, speak in tongues, teach, preach, and comfort. This power gives Christians the ability to hear the still small voice of Jesus and move in the supernatural.

It was revealed to me that I should say "Thank you Jesus" out loud at least once everyday of my life and tell others to do the same. We should get in the habit of saying Jesus often since he says in John 12:32, "If I be lifted up from the earth I will draw all [people] unto me." Jesus is lifted up by having faith in him and by calling on his name. To grow spiritually Christians must lift up the name Jesus in our prayers and conversations. In order for people to be healed and delivered we must lift up the name Jesus when we pray and worship. To pray for the sick and they get well and to rebuke the devil and make him flee and to speak in tongues to receive divine revelations, we must call on the name Jesus because he tells us in his Word not to deny his name (see Rev. 3:8).

There is also another reason to call on the name Jesus. The world is a hostile place. There is jealousy, resentment, persecution and rejection on every side. But Jesus promises to take care of us if we believe in him and speak his name out loud. Some of us have to confront evil everyday. "The devil walks about like a roaring lion seeking whom he may devour" (1 Pet. 5:8). Satan stays on our case. But Jesus promises to shield and protect us if we speak his name out loud in faith. So in order to get Holy Ghost power we must be obedient to receive it. That means we have to obey Jesus when he says through one of his prophets, "Call to me and I will answer you and tell you great and mighty things you do not know" (Jer. 33:3). He says through me, "Obey and pray."

Jesus says, "Whoever shall be ashamed of me in this adulterous and sinful generation, of them shall I be ashamed when I come in my glory with the holy angels" (Mk. 8:38).

Amazingly, Jesus says to me and to others, "You did not choose me, but I chose you and appointed you that you should go and bear fruit, and that your fruit should remain" (Jn. 15:16).

His Word says to me and to others, "My kindness shall not depart from you, neither shall the covenant of my peace be removed, for I will have mercy on you" (Is. 54:10).

Jesus says to me and to others, "I give you authority to tread on serpents and scorpions, and over all the power of the enemy: and nothing shall by any means hurt you" (Lk. 10:19).

Jesus says to me and to others, "These signs shall follow them that believe; In my name shall they cast out devils; they shall speak in new tongues; … they shall lay hands on the sick, and they shall recover" (Mk. 16: 17-18).

His Word says especially to me, "Remember not the former things, neither consider the things of old. Behold, I will do a new thing" (Is. 43:18-19a).

Jesus says to me and to others, "Go into all the world and preach the gospel to every creature" (Mk. 16:15). Why, because of "the power of his resurrection" (Phil. 3:10).

It was revealed to me that the Prophet Isaiah was a gospel writer based on verses in Chapter 53. My rendition of the Bible verses given to me from Isaiah 53, Romans 8:2, Revelation 5:12; 21:4, and John 1:29 follow:

Who hath believed our report?

And to whom is the arm of the Lord revealed? (v. 1)

For he shall grow up as a tender plant,

And as a root out of dry ground:

He hath no form of comeliness;

There is no beauty that we should desire him. (v. 2)

He is despised and rejected;

A man of sorrows and acquainted with grief:

We hid our faces from him;

He was despised,

And we esteemed him not. (v. 3)

Surely he hath borne our griefs,

And carried our sorrows:

Yet we esteemed him stricken,

Smitten of God, and afflicted. (v. 4)

But he was wounded for our transgressions,

He was bruised for our iniquities:

The chastisement of our peace was upon him;

And with his stripes we are healed. (v. 5)

All we like sheep have gone astray;

We have turned every one to his own way;

And he hath laid on himself

The iniquities of us all. (v. 6)

He was oppressed and afflicted,

Yet he opened not his mouth:

He is brought as a lamb to the slaughter,

And as a sheep before her shearers is dumb,

He opened not his mouth. (v. 7)

He was taken from prison and from judgment:

And who shall declare his generation?

For he was cut off out of the land of the living:

For the transgression of his people he was stricken. (v. 8)

He made his grave with the wicked,

And with the rich in his death;

For he had done no violence,

Neither was any deceit in his mouth. (v. 9)

Yet it pleased himself to be bruised;

He made his soul an offering for sin. (v. 10)

He hath poured out his soul unto death:

And made intercession for the transgressors. (v. 12)

We need to recall the resurrection

For worthy is the lamb that was slain (Rev. 5:12)

The lamb of God who takes away

The sins of the world (Jn. 1:29)

And makes us free

From the law of sin and death (Rom. 8:2)

Because of the resurrection.

We are to recall the resurrection,

And he will wipe away

All tears from our eyes (Rev. 21:4)

Because of the resurrection.

We are to recall the resurrection.

Recall with thanksgiving the resurrection.

Recall with great joy the resurrection.

Recall the resurrection.

The resurrection,

The resurrection...

CHAPTER 7

On occasion Jesus referred to himself as God. He said to the Gadarene demoniac he healed who wanted to follow him, "Go home to your friends and tell them how great things the Lord hath done for you and hath had compassion on you. And [being obedient] he went and began to publish how great things Jesus had done for him and the people did marvel" (Mk. 5:19-20).

Then there was the time Jesus healed ten lepers but only one came back to thank him. Jesus said, "Were there not ten cleansed? But where are the nine? There are not found that returned to give glory to God, save this stranger" (Lk. 17:17-18). Jesus was referring to himself as God since he did the healing.

But perhaps the clearest reference to himself as God occurred when Jesus healed Bartimaes, a man who was born blind. Jesus asked him, "Do you believe in the Son of God? He answered and said, Who is he, Lord, that I might believe in him? Jesus said, You have both seen him, and it is he that is talking with you. And he said, Lord, I believe. And he worshipped him" (Jn. 9:35-38). Jesus allowed the man to worship him and did not even attempt to stop him. If Jesus were not God he would have been guilty of blasphemy.

And, Jesus refers to himself as God in John 10:27 when he says, "My sheep hear my voice, and I know them, and they follow me," but especially when he says, "And lo, I am with you always, even unto the close of the age" (Mt. 28:20). Only God can speak of eternity as if reading the last chapter in a saga and closing the book.

But it has to be acknowledged that like Paul Jesus spoke in code too, on occasion, for practical reasons. He taught in parables saying to his disciples and the people around them, "Unto you it is given to know the mystery of the kingdom of God: but unto them that are without, all these things are done in parables: That seeing they may see, and not perceive; and hearing they may hear, and not understand; lest at any time they should be converted, and their sins should be forgiven them" (Mk. 4:11-12). Along the same lines Jesus says in Matthew 13:15, "For this people's heart is waxed gross, and their ears are dull of hearing, and their eyes they have closed; lest at any time they should see with their eyes, and hear with their ears, and should understand with their heart, and should be converted, and I should heal them." It is as though the incarnation watered down the wrath he had in the Old Testament. For example, he was angry with Adam and Eve for disobeying him in the Garden of Eden and bringing sin and death into the world even though in his mind he already had the plan of salvation (see Gen. 3:14-19).

He was angry with the original people he created for their wickedness and decided to send rain to destroy all life on earth with a flood except Noah and his family and two of every animal, bird and creeping thing (see Gen. 6:5-8).

He was angry with Moses for his disobedience. In Horeb the first time the people cried for water he told Moses to hit the rock and water would come out (see Ex. 17:1-7) and the second time in Meribah to speak to the rock, but Moses hit the rock the second time too (Num. 20:1-13) and, consequently, could not enter the Promised Land but had to go stand on Mount Nebo and view the land from a distance (Deut. 34:1-4).

Angry with Korah for rebelling against Moses, he split open the ground and swallowed up him and his family (see Num. 16:31-3) in an earthquake.

He was angry with the Israelites for complaining against him and Moses and murmuring about the manna he provided for them to eat, so he killed a lot of them with poisonous snakes (see Num. 21:5-6).

He was angry with Uzzah for putting his hand on the Ark of the Covenant after he had said no one should touch it and killed him on the spot (see 2 Sam. 6:6-7).

He was angry with David for taking Uriah the Hittite's wife, Bethsheba, and having him killed (2 Sam. 11:4, 14-17).

He was angry with Saul for being impatient and burning incense himself instead of waiting for Samuel the prophet and priest (1 Sam. 13:5-14).

He was angry with Hezekiah for showing off his wealth to men from Babylon, a country that would later take the children of Israel into captivity (2 Kin. 20:12-19).

He was angry with Manasseh for shedding so much innocent blood (see 2 Kin. 21:16) during the fifty-five years he reigned as King of Judah in Jerusalem (see 2 Kin. 21:1).

He was angry with the Israelites for their disobedience and for "every man doing that which was right in his own eyes" (Judg. 17:6) and allowed them to be taken into captivity by King Nebuchadnezzar of Babylon (2 Kin. 25:1-21).

He was angry when he told the Prophet Malachi to tell Israel to "bring all the tithes into the storehouse, that there may be meat in [his] house" (Mal. 3:10) because the people were robbing him in their tithes and offerings (Mal. 3:8) by putting defiled food on his altar (Mal. 1:7).

He was angry when he called Simon Peter Satan for trying to talk him out of going to the cross (Mt. 16:23); and when he whipped the moneychangers out of the temple for turning his house of prayer into a den of thieves (see Mk. 11:15-17); and when he had to cast the demon out of the young man because his disciples were not able to (Mk. 9:14-29). He was furious with the Pharisees calling them hypocrites, snakes, and blind fools (see Mt. 23:13-36) for laying heavy burdens on men's shoulders (Mt. 23:4) and neglecting "the weightier matters of the law: judgment, mercy and faith: [saying] these you ought to have done, and not to leave the other undone" (Mt. 23:23). He was angry at the fig tree for not having fruit on it when he wanted something to eat—even though it was not the time for figs—and cursed it drying it to the very root (Mk. 11:12-14), 20-21); and when he called Cleopas and his companion fools for not believing the prophets who foretold his death and resurrection (see Lk. 24:13-27). Luke 24:27 is especially noteworthy. Luke says, "And beginning at Moses and all the prophets, he expounded unto them in all the Scriptures the things concerning himself."

But although watered down his anger is wrath just the same, which is where preaching the gospel of the cross comes in: to keep the wrath of God at bay at least long enough for more people to repent and turn to him before he opens the seven seals letting the four horsemen of the apocalypse ride instead of trot like they are now (see Rev. 6:1-17).

That being said, Jesus spoke in code when he "perceived that [the people] would come and take him by force, to make him a king" (Jn. 6:15), and when he talked about himself to keep from sounding like a braggart. Proverbs 27:2 reads, "Let another man praise thee, and not thine own mouth, a stranger, and not thine own lips."

The best example for me of when Jesus speaks in code about his being God is a passage in the fifth chapter of John's gospel. He said to some Jews in Jerusalem who were arguing with him,

> Verily, verily, I say unto you, The Son can do nothing of himself, but what he seeth the Father do: for what things soever he doeth, these also doeth the Son likewise. For the Father loveth the Son, and showeth him all things that himself doeth: and he will show him greater works than these, that ye may marvel. For as the Father raiseth up the dead, and quickeneth them; even so the Son quickeneth whom he will. For the Father judgeth no man, but hath committed all judgment unto the Son. *That all men should honor the Son, even as they honor the Father* [emphasis mine]. He that honoreth not the Son honoreth not the Father which hath sent him. Verily, verily, I say unto you, He that heareth my word, and believeth on him that sent me, hath everlasting life, and shall not come into condemnation; but is passed from death unto life. Verily, verily, I say unto you, The hour is coming, and now is, when the dead shall hear the voice of the Son of God: and they

that hear shall live. For as the Father hath life in himself; so hath he given to the Son to have life in himself; And hath given him authority to execute judgment also, because he is the Son of man. Marvel not at this: for the hour is coming, in the which all that are in the graves shall hear his voice, And shall come forth; they that have done good, unto the resurrection of life; and they that have done evil, unto the resurrection of damnation. I can of mine own self do nothing: as I hear, I judge: and my judgment is just; because I seek not mine own will but the will of the Father which hath sent me. (Jn. 5:19-30)

The Holy Ghost gave me permission to paraphrase my interpretation of the above passage. Remember, Jesus spoke those words over 2000 years ago. He expects us to have grown spiritually since then and be able to hear his voice and articulate the interpretation of his words for today.

19.   Truly, truly, I say to you, I do what I see for myself.

20.   I love my creation and will do greater works so that you may marvel.

21.   I raise the dead and make alive whomever I want.

22.   I came into the world the first time to save, but I am coming back to judge.

23.   All men should honor me for I am worthy of honor.

24.   Truly, truly, I say to you, They who believe in me have everlasting life and will not come into condemnation but are passed from death to life.

25.   Truly, truly, I say to you, The hour is coming, and now is when the dead will hear my voice: and they that hear will live.

26.   For I am the author of life

27.   And have authority to execute judgment also, because I am God.

28.   Marvel not at this: for the hour is coming, in which all that are in the grave will hear my voice

29.   And will come forth: they that have done good to the resurrection of life; and they that have done evil to the resurrection of damnation.

48

30. I shall not do anything without thinking first then speaking my thoughts out loud so that my Holy Spirit shall hear and act.

Another passage that I was given permission to paraphrase my interpretation is John 17, the entire chapter, which reads as follows:

These words spake Jesus, and lifted up his eyes to heaven, and said, Father, the hour is come; glorify thy Son, that thy Son also may glorify thee: As thou hast given him power over all flesh, that he should give eternal life to as many as thou hast given him. And this is life eternal, that they might know thee the only true God, and Jesus Christ, whom thou hast sent. I have glorified thee on the earth: I have finished the work which thou gavest me to do. And now, O Father, *glorify thou me with thine own self with the glory which I had with thee before the world was* [emphasis mine]. I have manifested thy name unto the men which thou gavest me out of the world: thine they were, and thou gavest them me; and they have kept thy word. Now they have known that all things whatsoever thou hast given me are of thee. For I have given unto them the words which thou gavest me; and they have received them, and have known surely that I came out from thee, and they have believed that thou didst send me. I pray for them; I pray not for the world, but for them which thou hast given me; for they are thine. And all mine are thine, and thine are mine; and I am glorified in them. And now I am no more in the world, but these are in the world, and I come to thee. Holy Father, keep through thine own name those whom thou hast given me, that they may be one, as we are. While I was with them in the world, I kept them in thy name: those that thou gavest me I have kept, and none of them is lost, but the son of perdition; that the Scripture might be fulfilled. And now come I to thee; and these things I speak in the world, that they might have my joy fulfilled in themselves. I have given them thy word; and the world hath hated them, because they are not of the world, even as I am not of the world. I pray not that thou shouldest take them out of the world, but that thou shouldest keep them from the evil. They are not of the world, even as I am not of the world. Sanctify them through thy truth: thy word is truth. As thou hast sent me into the world, even so have I also sent them into the world. And for their sakes I sanctify myself, that they also might be sanctified through the truth. Neither pray I for these alone, but for them also which shall believe on me through their word; That they all may be one; as thou, Father, art in me, and I in thee, that they also may be one in us; that the world may believe that thou hast sent me. And the glory which thou gavest me I have given them; that they may be one, even as we are one: I in them, and thou in me, that they may be made perfect in one; and that the world may know that thou hast sent me, and hast loved them, as thou hast loved me. Father, I will that they also, whom thou hast given me, be with me where I am; that they may behold my glory, which thou hast given me: for thou lovedst me before the foundation of the world. O righteous Father, the world hath not known thee: but I have known thee, and these have known that thou hast sent me. And I have declared unto them thy name, and will declare it: that the love wherewith thou hast loved me may be in them, and I in them. (Jn. 17:1-26)

My interpretation begins here:

1. These words spake Jesus to himself as he lifted up his eyes to heaven, The hour is come for me to be glorified:

2. As I have power over all flesh to give eternal life to as many as believe in me.

3. And this is life eternal, that they might know me, Jesus Christ, the only true God.

50

4. I have glorified myself on earth and have finished the work I came down here to do.

5. And now I glorify mine own self with the glory that I had before the world was.

6. I have manifested my name unto men in the world who were always mine; and they have kept my word.

7. Now they have known that all things are of me.

8. For I have given unto them my words; and they have received them, and have known surely that I came from above, and they have believed me.

9. I focus on them: I focus not on the world, but on them for they are mine.

10. All are mine, and I am glorified in them.

11. And now I am no more in the world, but these are in the world, and I go above. So I will keep through my own name those whom I have that they may be one with me.

12. While I was with them in the world, I kept them in my name: those that are mine I have kept, and none of them is lost, but the son of perdition; that the Scripture might be fulfilled.

13. And now I go above; and these things I speak in the world, that they might have my joy fulfilled in themselves.

14. I have given them my word; and the world hath hated them, because they are not of the world, even as I am not of the world.

15. I feel not that I should take them out of the world, but that I should keep them from the evil.

16. They are not of the world, even as I am not of the world.

17. I sanctify them through my truth: my word is truth.

18. As I have come into the world, even so have I also sent them into the world.

19. And for their sakes I sanctify myself, that they also might be sanctified through the truth.

(Occasionally Jesus slips out of the code and verse 19 is a prime example. He did not say that for their sakes the Father sanctified him but that he sanctified himself.)

20. Neither speak I for these alone, but for them also which shall believe on me through their word;

21. That they all may be one; that they also may be one in me; that the world may believe that I am from above.

22. And the glory which I have I have given them; that they may be one with me:

23. I in them, that they may be made perfect in one; and that the world may know that I am from above, and hast loved them as myself.

24. I will that they also, whom I have, be with me where I am; that they may behold my glory, which I have had before the foundation of the world.

25. O, the world hath not known me: but I know myself and that I am from above.

26. And I have declared unto them my name, and will declare it: that the love wherewith I have loved may be in them, and I in them.

At the end of this "Jesus specifically again" chapter, I was given a word to help readers understand more fully how to see Jesus as God. Hear what thus saith the Lord to me: "Every time 'Son of God' is read in the Bible or heard from the pulpit, think 'Flesh of God.' 'Son' is my 'Flesh.'" This concept is so simple yet has not been taught until now. For some reason God wanted me to write these buzz words for the New Millennium. He, God, called his flesh Son and named his flesh Jesus, that means Savior. The Word was made flesh (Jn. 1:14) for death. Jesus despised the shame of the cross (Heb. 12:2) where his scrotum rested on a rusty spike.

CHAPTER 8

On occasion Jesus talks about his Holy Spirit directly. "It is written in the prophets, And they shall be all taught of God. Every man therefore that hath heard, and hath learned of the Father, cometh unto me" (Jn. 6:45), saying that when he teaches it is his Holy Spirit. The Spirit renews the mind (see Eph. 4:23).

Because of the incarnation Jesus had to explain the work of his Holy Spirit in a simple way that was still complex such as, "The Comforter, which is the Holy Ghost, whom the Father will send in my name, shall teach you all things, and bring all things to your remembrance, whatsoever *I* have said unto you" [emphasis mine] (Jn. 14:26). For "These signs shall follow them that believe; In my name shall they cast out devils; they shall speak in new tongues; ... they shall lay hands on the sick, and they shall recover" (Mk. 16:17-18).

It is his Holy Spirit that "sounded" the Word at creation, that performs miracles, heals the sick, casts out demons, and "sounds" the "tongues of fire" available to those with the gift of tongues since Pentecost (see Acts 2:3-4). When Jesus tells his disciples then and now to "Heal the sick, cleanse the lepers, raise the dead, [and] cast out devils" (Mt. 10:8) he is promising us Holy Ghost power for successfully completing the tasks. And since he says to us, "I will never leave you nor forsake you" (Heb. 13:5) he is saying his Holy Spirit is capable of being everywhere with everyone at once. Statements like "Heaven and earth will pass away, but my words will never pass away" (Mt. 24:35) and "Lo, I am with you always, even unto the close of the age" (Mt. 28:20b) indicate that his Holy Spirit transcends time and space.

More often than not Jesus himself muddies the waters in explaining his identity like when he says, "My food is to do the will of Him who sent Me, and to finish His work" (Jn. 4:34). Two thousand plus years ago he had to paint such a picture of himself so that he would not alienate even more people than he did. However, time brings about a change. Christians are supposed to know better now since God no longer dwells in tents or stone buildings but in the temples of our hearts. We are to hear his Word and believe. But the question was asked, "How shall they believe in him of whom they have not heard? And how shall they hear without a preacher? And how shall they preach, except they be sent?" (Rom. 10:14b-15a). This causes me to reflect on my own call to pulpit ministry.

Years ago in the 1980s I was lying in bed one night sound asleep when I thought I heard my maternal grandfather, James William McKinley Carr, call my name. He said, "Jo! Jo!" Now Daddy McKinley had been dead for many years. I sat straight up in bed and said, "Huh?" But when I realized nobody was there, I lay back down and went back to sleep.

A year later the same thing happened again only that time I realized it was not Daddy McKinley. I had already read the Bible cover-to-cover a few times and was familiar with the passage in 1 Samuel 3 where the boy Samuel thought Eli the priest was calling him, but it turned out to be the Lord.

After hearing my name called a third time in 1991, I tried to rationalize what had happened to me and wondered if God really called women to preach or were we called to minister in some other way. Then I remembered John 20 where Mary Magdalene was at the tomb weeping.

Jesus appeared to Mary Magdalene first after he rose from the dead (Mk. 16:9). He stood over her and called her by name (Jn. 20:16). She turned and recognized him but he told her not to touch him because he had not yet ascended back to heaven but to go and tell his disciples that he is alive (Jn. 20:17).

The word gospel means good news. The good news is Jesus rose from the dead with all power (Mt. 28:18); the grave could not hold him. He had told his disciples before he was killed, "After I am risen, I will go before you into Galilee" (Mk. 14:28). After he rose he had a woman spread the news first. Now if that is not calling a woman to preach, I do not know what is.

Still I did not want to accept the idea that God was calling me to preach. I thought I was too glamorous to be a preacher and decided to go into show business. But my two-year stint working for my celebrity cousin, Oprah Winfrey, in the late 1980s proved to be disastrous for me even though I am glad now that I briefly worked for her.

I had two Master's degrees and a Ph.D. in English in the late 1980s and enjoyed teaching. So I decided to go back to the college classroom as a teacher. Regarding my call, initially I decided to be an evangelist and not a pastor with all the responsibilities of running a church. That way I could both teach and preach.

Evangelical means preaching the lessons of the New Testament, so I started forming my theology. The Bible taught me to believe that every worship service should be a ceremony of thanksgiving to Jesus for salvation and the gift of eternal life.

I also saw in the Word that God has concern for the world's agonies and turmoil. I was suffering from many things back then both emotional and physical and plunged into Bible reading and prayer for comfort. The Psalms are especially good for soothing hurt feelings.

I discovered early in my spiritual journey that suffering is a part of life and that there is a blessing in suffering if it is done right. For example, the Word says, "The Spirit of Christ … did signify when it testified beforehand the sufferings of Christ, and the glory that should follow" (1 Pet. 1:11). This says to me that if we suffer for something we do not bring on ourselves, there is a blessing coming that equals the intensity of the suffering.

Support for my theory is in several other verses. Psalm 126:5-6 says, "They that sow in tears shall reap in joy. He that goeth forth weeping, bearing precious seed, shall doubtless come again with rejoicing, bringing his sheaves with him." This means that suffering with Jesus yields a blessing that turns sadness into joy.

A psalm of Moses says, "Make us glad according to the days wherein thou hast afflicted us and the years wherein we have seen evil" (Ps. 90:15). This means for every day we have suffered, Lord, make us equally glad. And even though Moses did not make it to the Promised Land, which probably hurt him badly, I am sure he was glad the others did.

The Prophet Zechariah speaking for God writes, "Turn you to the stronghold, ye prisoners of hope: even today do I declare that I will render double unto thee" (Zech. 9:12). To me this means that the Lord will bless us twice for each woe we endure.

But the best proof of suffering's yielding a blessing is in the story of Job. After he had lost his property (Job 1:14-17), his children (Job 1:18-19), and his health (Job 2:7), he was restored. "The Lord gave Job twice as much as he had before" (Job 42:10b). "So the Lord blessed the latter end of Job more than his beginning" (Job 42:12a). "After this Job lived an hundred and forty [more] years … [and] died being old and full of days" (Job 42:16a, 17a).

And regarding the suffering I experienced, I feel "It is good for me that I have been afflicted, that I might learn [the Lord's] statutes" (Ps. 119:71). I must admit, the suffering I endured made me feel good about being an over-comer.

Even though a great deal of suffering is caused by people's intentional alienation from God, it is comforting to know that the Lord is longsuffering and willing to forgive our sins and iniquities and remember them no more (Heb. 10:17).

Preachers are called to teach people how to live a life of faith. I try to do that and shape attitudes. Starting with myself I try to treat people the way I would want to be treated believing that we are to practice forgiveness, serve others, show mercy, have compassion, and obey God.

Jesus gives a good example of how Christians are supposed to act in a passage in Matthew that says, "I was hungry and ye gave me meat: I was thirsty, and ye gave me drink: I was a stranger, and ye took me in: Naked and ye clothed me: I was sick and ye visited me: I was in prison and ye came unto me" (Mt. 25:35-36), for "Inasmuch as ye have done it unto one of the least of these my brethren, ye have done it unto me" (Mt. 25:30).

I believe the main problem in society today is that people want to be self-sufficient and in control. They do not want God intruding on their notions of how things should or should not be done. They resist the Bible and substitute secular paraphrases of it or worldly doctrines to support their choices. But the Scripture is here to stay. Jesus says in Matthew 24:35, "Heaven and earth shall pass away, but my words shall not pass away."

I preach that it is through obedience and service that we Christians experience the rewards of our faith. Obedience to God is for our protection "For we wrestle not against flesh and blood, but against principalities, against powers, against the rulers of the darkness of this world" (Eph. 6:12). Furthermore, "To obey is better than sacrifice, and to hearken than the fat of rams" (1 Sam. 15:22). When we obey we show respect for "the God in whose hand [our] breath is" (Dan. 5:23).

We experience God's handiwork in nature and the things that grow. Our food, clothes and shelter all come from the earth. Gold, silver, precious jewels, oil, minerals, and electricity name only a few. God says all the "silver and gold [are] mine" (1 Kin. 20:3) and I own "the cattle [on] a thousand hills" (Ps. 50:10).

We experience God in the miracle of birth, in healing and reconciliation. We sense the presence of the Holy Spirit in our feelings of joy, peace, love, and satisfaction in a job well done.

But I believe the greatest feeling we experience is that of comfort at those times when only comfort will do: when we are sad, lonely, depressed, angry, afraid, and just plain tired. Yet "though outwardly we perish," in Jesus we are "renewed day by day" (2 Cor. 4:16) through his generous Holy Spirit. And, to me the experience of communing with God through prayer is the highest form of worship.

The Psalmist says, "When I consider thy heavens, the work of thy fingers, the moon and the stars which thou hast ordained; What is man that thou art mindful of him? and the son of man, that thou visitest him? For thou hast made him a little lower than the angels, and hast crowned him with glory and honor" (Ps. 8:3-5).

I cannot help but marvel at the wonders of creation. We humans are insignificant in the midst of the sea and helpless in the face of a storm. However, we are privileged to be able to see the beauty in lightning, funnel clouds, and sea billows before their devastating results.

So I, a woman, know I was called to preach. Reluctantly I answered the call and now that I have surrendered to God, I am satisfied and more at peace. But my main point is if the wind and the sea obey Jesus (Mk. 4:41), who am I not to?

Now the call to preach means several things to me, so I shall summarize how it all began to help others learn what the call sounds like and because repetition teaches irrespective of the subject. So, again, Jesus called my name on three separate occasions to preach his gospel but like the boy Samuel, I did not recognize his voice at first. I thought I was dreaming the first time and hearing things the second. But the third time I realized that it was Jesus calling me into the ministry.

I had heard Jesus' voice when I was seven years old. He comforted me when I was lonesome for my mother. My parents were divorced and my paternal grandparents raised my brother and me.

When I was fourteen I read the King James Version of the Bible like a novel everyday and discovered that Jesus even spoke to me back then. For example, one day I was led to memorize 2 Timothy 2:15. It says, "Study to show thyself approved unto God, a workman that needeth not to be ashamed rightly dividing the word of truth." So my being in college twenty-five years and earning a Bachelor's degree, three Master's and a Ph.D. was something I felt called to do. Like many of my Jewish friends, I consider study a form of worship.

After hearing the call to preach the third time I doubted it and told God he could not be serious. I even suggested to him that I was too glamorous to be a preacher. That is the time he told me I did not have to change my personality, that he would use my style to draw people to him and grow churches. I argued some more saying that my voice was not right and that because of my Southern accent people would not take me seriously. Then the Spirit led me to the Bible passage about Moses and his reluctance to go tell Pharaoh to let the children of

Israel leave Egypt. Moses told God he was not a good speaker but God said to him, "Who made man's mouth?" (see Ex. 4:10-11).

Then what Jesus said to a few of his disciples on the Mount of Olives came to mind. He said, "Ye shall be brought before rulers and kings for my sake, for a testimony against them. And the gospel must first be published among all nations. But when they shall lead you, and deliver you up, take no thought beforehand what ye shall speak, neither do ye premeditate: but whatsoever shall be given you in that hour, that speak ye: for it is not ye that speak, but the Holy Ghost" (Mk. 13:9-11). So questioning God showed me that doubt is necessary for spiritual growth.

After Jesus called me to preach he also called me to tune. Tuning is a form of preaching in the Black Tradition. It is half talking and half singing at the end of the message—during the celebration—and sounds like a more conservative form of rap music although some preachers "whoop," which is just as dramatic and theatrical.

A man by the name of Mr. John W. Stokes taught me how to tune. He was a member of Ninth Street United Methodist Church in Covington, Kentucky. I attended that church when I moved from Milwaukee, Wisconsin, to Cincinnati, Ohio. Mr. Stokes would pray practically every Sunday and he would begin the same way every time so I ended up memorizing the front part of his prayer. One day the Spirit told me to tune verses of Scripture when I preach and that is how I got started, imitating Mr. Stokes. He died many years ago, but I think of him often because Mr. John W. Stokes taught me how to tune.

Most of my "God-thought" and "God-talk" come from Scripture and divine revelation. One day God gave me a word about how to explain the Trinity that made sense to me. God the Father is original thought, God the Son is the articulated Word, and God the Holy Spirit is activity or deed. Put more simply, God is thought, Word, and deed whose name is Jesus.

The revelation also made it clear to me that men and women are equal in God's sight because Jesus was a man and a woman gave birth to him. When God

59

decided to come to earth, he used a woman to get here which is what equalized the value of the sexes. And, actually, The Virgin Mary is the first preacher of the Gospel—male or female—as proclaimed in her song in Luke 1:46-55.

I learned from Scripture and the Holy Ghost that Jesus is the divine revelation of himself, so John 1:1-3 and 14 marks the foundation of my theology. John 1:5 explains how people initially could not comprehend Jesus and many are still unable to grasp hold of him today. But his grace and mercy is still leading many of us to keep on preaching the gospel of the cross. My call inspires me to preach who Jesus is, his death on the cross for the forgiveness of sin, and his resurrection from the dead with all power (see Mt. 28:18). The Apostle Paul writes that he is determined not to know anything save Jesus Christ and him crucified (1 Cor. 2:2), and that is good. But I say I am determined not to know anything save Jesus Christ, him crucified and him resurrected with all power, which, to me, is better. Jesus is not on the cross anymore or in the tomb but is back where he started with his original thoughts, spoken words and actions.

Jesus walked the earth and went about doing good (Acts 10:30). He died for our sins (1 Cor. 15:13), rose from the dead (Rom. 14:9), went back to heaven (Jn. 3:13), and his spoken words are the root power of himself (Rom. 15:12). So in addition to being given a definition of the Trinity in Bible verses—that God is thought, Word, and deed in the person of Jesus—my call says that in my preaching I am not to make a distinction in the Godhead. Jesus has all power in heaven and in earth and told me to "Go ye, therefore, and teach all nations … to observe all things whatsoever I have commanded you" (Mt. 28:19-20). God revealed to me that he deferred to his spoken Word after the resurrection and for me to take him from flesh back to Spirit directly and in a straightforward way whenever I preach or write or teach, if nobody else does.

Referring to the Holy Spirit Jesus says in John 15:26, "When the Comforter comes, whom I will send to you from the Father, even the Spirit of truth who proceeds from the Father, He will testify of me." This verse is saying that after deferring to the Word the Holy Spirit confirms the Word as the

60

foundation of God who is Jesus. Furthermore, John 7:38 says that Jesus spoke of his Spirit, which they who believe in him would receive after his resurrection: for the Holy Ghost was not yet given; because Jesus was not yet glorified—since the incarnation, that is.

So I preach Jesus Christ, period. I preach Jesus because nothing in the world would mean anything to me if death and the grave were all there is. Our sins are forgiven and we have eternal life because of Jesus and his work on the cross and his resurrection from the dead with all power.

Praying is also as much a part of my call as preaching. I am a pastor and have a Prayer Language (which is speaking in tongues) that I use for heavy-duty deliverance ministry, when praying for the sick, waiting with the dying and for healing and comfort.

I am grateful that Jesus called me to preach the Word in season and out (2 Tim. 4:2) and to "go into all the world and preach the gospel to every creature" (Mk. 16:15). I was even given a personal interpretation of The Ten Commandments (see Ex. 20:1-17). As Jesus says, "He that hath ears to hear, let him hear" (Lk. 8:8).

I. We should not worship other gods like the stars, nature or fertility gods but worship "Jesus only" (Mk. 9:8).

II. We should not make a god out of things like money, power, sex, food, sports, ourselves or other people.

III. We should not disrespect Jesus' name by using it flippantly or with profanity.

IV. We should remember the Sabbath day—the day Jesus rested after creating the world—and rest ourselves in some way on that day.

V. We should love and respect our parents who are responsible for our lives and appreciate what they did for us.

VI.   We should not kill irreverently. If we hunt we should respect our game. If we are soldiers, we should ask God to have mercy on us and on our enemies.

VII.   We should not be unfaithful in marriage.

VIII.   We should not take what belongs to someone else.

IX.   We should not cause harm to people by lying on them.

X.   We should not be jealous of what other people have to the extent that we would try to take it away from them.

And we should know that when Jesus states the first and greatest commandment which is love the Lord our God with all our heart, soul, strength and mind and the second which is to love our neighbor as ourselves (see Mt. 22:37-40) he is commanding us to try and live holy lives.

Once we hear what "thus saith the Lord" (Ezek. 17:3), our job is to obey. Obedience is the truest form of worship. We can go to church every Sunday and sing and pray all day long, but if we are not obedient, we are not truly worshiping God.

Again, in Scripture when Samuel was a boy, Eli the priest was raising him. Samuel was in bed one night and heard a voice call his name three times. He got up and went to Eli because he thought Eli was calling him when it was the Lord (see 1 Sam. 3:1-15). Well, something similar happened to me. I was called three times by Jesus to preach his gospel. I answered the call in 1991 and, as the old hymn goes, I had decided to follow Jesus and there was no turning back.

Still, I had my doubts, so I attended seminary and graduated from United Theological Seminary in Dayton, Ohio, in 1997. I had a rough time after that in a denomination I do not wish to mention that I left. Thankfully I was received into the African Methodist Episcopal Church (AME) and was ordained an Itinerant Elder on November 17, 2005. Now I am pastoring "A New Work" voted "A New Church" (Kosciusko AME Church, 312 Tipton Street, Kosciusko, Mississippi 39090) at the 138th Session of the North Mississippi Annual Conference of the Eighth Episcopal District, held August 22-26, 2012, at St. Matthew AME Church in Greenville, Rev. Larry L. Story, Pastor. My Presiding Elder is Rev. Archie R. Smith of the Greenville-Greenwood District, and the Eighth District's new Bishop is The Right Reverend Julius H. McAllister, Sr.

John 2:17 says, "The zeal for thine house hath eaten me up," and applies to me. I know firsthand the joy of serving as a pastor and am glad about the verse where Jesus says, "the gates of hell shall not prevail against [his church]" (Mt. 16:18).

But the real Church is not the building; it is the people. Since the resurrection, believers are now the flesh of God. We are the body of Christ, an extension of Jesus who is the head. I preach Jesus Christ because Jesus died on the cross for the sins of the world and rose from the dead with all power. I was called by Jesus to pray, teach, preach, listen, pastor, and obey, so I am determined to serve him in those ways the best I can.

CHAPTER 9

The following passage capsules the reason I was told to write down and share the Bible verses given to me:

> Behold, the days come, saith the Lord, that I will make a new covenant with the house of Israel and with the house of Judah: Not according to the covenant that I made with their fathers in the day that I took them by the hand to bring them out of the land of Egypt; which my covenant they broke, although I was a husband unto them, saith the Lord: But this shall be the covenant that I will make with the house of Israel; After those days, saith the Lord, I will put my law in their inward parts, and write it in their hearts; and will be their God, and they shall be my people. And they shall teach no more every man his neighbor, and every man his brother, saying, Know the Lord: for they shall all know me, from the least of them unto the greatest of them, saith the Lord. (Jer. 31:31-34)

To me Jesus lamented about his preachers—including me—being stuck in the old covenant not knowing his Holy Spirit because of the incarnation and directed me to write down what he gives me to help set the record straight. Emphasis is placed on, "That I may know him, and the power of his resurrection" (Phil. 3:10). So as an obedient servant, this is my understanding of the Holy Spirit from before creation until now as revealed in the Bible verses given to me. "He who has an ear, let him hear what the Spirit says" (Rev. 2:7).

The Holy Spirit is a person, Jesus, and not a thing. Jesus refers to the Holy Spirit as "he"—talking about himself—although the Greek is neuter, meaning neither male nor female. And that is accurate because Jesus is pure spirit again now since the resurrection, like he was before creation.

The Holy Spirit is a person with power and influence (Acts 1:8) who dwells with us (Jn. 14:17), meaning he will come and live in our hearts and minds if we ask him to so that he can teach us. When we read the Bible he helps us understand and remember what he says in his Word (Jn. 14:26).

The most important action of the Holy Spirit is he bears witness of himself, Jesus (Jn. 15:26), testifying of who he, Jesus, is. Because we are born in sin and are sinners naturally, the Holy Spirit convinces us that we need him, Jesus (Jn. 16:8). He tells us what is right and wrong (Jn. 16:13) and guides and directs us in the way we should go if we let him. So whenever the Holy Spirit speaks of Jesus, he is talking about himself and vice versa.

Christians have the Bible that was written by men who were inspired by the Holy Spirit for he speaks through the Scriptures (Acts 1:16; 2 Pet. 1:21). Heaven and earth will pass away but his Word will never pass away (Lk. 21:33).

The Holy Spirit calls ministers (Acts 13:2) and other Kingdom workers (Acts 13:4) by name to do certain jobs for him. He also warns us (Acts 16:6-7). Whenever we say, "My mind said to me" or "Something told me not to do that," the Holy Spirit is speaking to us. Jesus says, "My Spirit will guide you into all truth … and show you things to come" (Jn. 16:13).

The Holy Spirit intercedes for us (Rom. 8:26). That means he talks to himself on our behalf. His actions are shrouded in mystery but he will reveal himself to us if we go to church to hear the Word preached, pray and study the Scriptures for ourselves and are open to his supernatural manifestations. For example, the Transfiguration was a supernatural event Jesus allowed Peter, James and John to witness. They were on a high mountain with Jesus when there appeared with him Moses and Elijah. But what happened to Jesus is what is significant. The Word says, "His raiment became shining, exceeding white as snow; so as no fuller on earth can white them" (Mk. 9:3) (see Mk. 9:1-13). A fuller is a person who uses a soap that is an alkali made from ashes of certain plants for cleansing new cloth (see Mal. 3:2) (Bryant 182). This passage is about a supernatural manifestation where Jesus showed those three disciples another aspect of his glory. But this passage—more than any other one for me—supports what Jesus means when he says he is God of the living and not the dead (see Mk.

12:27). Even though Elijah was taken up to heaven in a chariot of fire (see 2 Kin. 2:11), Deuteronomy 34:5 says Moses died. No one was able to find his grave because the Lord buried him (see Deut. 34:6). However, the dead live because Moses was with Elijah and Jesus on the Mount of Transfiguration. That lets me know that the supernatural is inherent in the Holy Ghost.

The Holy Spirit has a personality we can relate to because he has his own will (1 Cor. 2:10-13; Rom. 15:30). He can love; he can hate, and his feelings can be hurt. We know this because he loves us, he hates sin, and we hurt his feelings when we are disobedient.

Because the Holy Spirit is a person, he can be lied to, tempted (Acts 5:3-4, 9) and rejected like we do to each other (Acts 7:51). And, he can be grieved (Eph. 4:30) and even outraged (Heb. 10:29) when we refuse to believe in him.

The Holy Spirit is the activity or movement of Jesus and not believing that is dangerous because it is a form of blasphemy (Mt. 12:31), which is speaking carelessly of God. Another form of blasphemy is to do what Job's wife told him to do and that is curse God (Job 2:9).

But the worst blasphemy is unbelief and bragging about it. Jesus says, "He that is not with me is against me; and he that gathereth not with me scattereth abroad. Wherefore I say unto you, All manner of sin and blasphemy shall be forgiven unto men: but the blasphemy against the Holy Ghost shall not be forgiven unto men. And whosoever speaketh a word against the Son of man, it shall be forgiven him: but whosoever speaketh against the Holy Ghost, it shall not be forgiven him, neither in this world, neither in the world to come" (Mt. 12:30-32). One reason for that is his Holy Ghost is the energy that enabled Jesus to raise himself from the dead somewhat like the strength humans and other animals have to get up on our feet when the Holy Ghost wakes us out of sleep.

So Jesus teaches that the sin of unbelief is the worst blasphemy and that blasphemy against the Holy Spirit—meaning saying there is no Holy Spirit—is the only sin that cannot be forgiven (Mt. 12:31). It makes sense, because how can a person seek forgiveness from someone he believes does not exist? That translates into not wanting forgiveness in the first place.

Another point that comes to mind is some non-Christians resent being told they are not going to heaven. But unbelief in Jesus says the person does not want to go to heaven. I mean, why would anyone who does not believe in Jesus want to spend eternity with him?

But to me the most significant characteristic of the Holy Spirit is his identity (Mt. 28:19; 2 Cor. 13:14), because Jesus speaks of the Holy Spirit as his other self (Jn. 14:16-17). To have the Holy Spirit is to have Jesus (Rom. 8:9-12). God is Spirit—except during the incarnation when he was both Spirit and flesh—and he can and will come and live in us (Jn. 4:24).

To be born again is to believe that God the Father, God the Son, and God the Holy Spirit are one person whose name is Jesus. "If we confess our sins, he is faithful and just to forgive us our sins, and to cleanse us from all unrighteousness" (1 Jn. 1:9). So we say, "Lord, be merciful to me a sinner" and "Jesus Christ, I need you," which signifies that we are born again.

Another activity of the Holy Spirit is that we can be "filled with him" (Acts 4:31). We can feel him and he can cause us to speak in tongues (Acts 10:44-48), which is a gift he gives to some people (1 Cor. 12:8-10). We do not all have the same gifts but everybody has at least one gift of the Spirit. Everyone alive has the gift of breath for the Word says, "man became a living soul" (Gen. 2:7) when the breath of God entered his body—man meaning humankind, that is. This explains why we cannot hold our breath long enough to stop breathing and die. And we cannot start breathing again on our own once the breath stops. Natural inhaling and exhaling are strictly under the purview of the Holy Spirit.

What Christians should realize is our body is the temple of the Holy Spirit (1 Cor. 6:19), so we should be careful not to willfully sin in thought, word, and deed against God's divine majesty provoking most justly his wrath and indignation, as stated in "The General Confession" of "The Lord's Supper" in the *African Methodist Episcopal Church Hymnal* (798).

67

Again, the Holy Spirit is the activity or movement of God and Trinitarian in terms of what he is called in the Bible. The Holy Spirit was not always called the Holy Spirit. His original title is the Spirit of God. Genesis 1:1-2 reads, "In the beginning God created the heaven and the earth. And the earth was without form, and void; and darkness was upon the face of the deep. And the *Spirit of God* [emphasis mine] moved upon the face of the waters." These two verses are the first two verses in the Old Testament and the beginning of the Bible. So in it we see starting out that God's Spirit has always been, even before God spoke and created the world and was originally called the Spirit of God.

Later on we read in Leviticus 19:2 that God said, "You shall be holy for I the Lord your God am holy." And in Isaiah 63:10 the prophet says the children of Israel "rebelled and vexed his Holy Spirit." So here we see a change from being called the Spirit of God to the Holy Spirit.

Then in the New Testament Matthew 1:18 says this: "Now the birth of Jesus Christ was on this wise: When his mother Mary was espoused to Joseph, before they came together, she was found with child of the Holy Ghost." What happened was, the angel of the Lord had to appear to Joseph and speak to him, because Joseph had thought about putting Mary away when he found out she was pregnant and knew he had not been with her. So the angel said, "Joseph, thou son of David, fear not to take unto thee Mary thy wife; for that which is conceived in her is of the Holy Ghost" (Mt. 1:20). And here we see yet another change in what the Spirit is called. That is why I say the Holy Spirit is himself Trinitarian because he is called the Spirit of God, one, the Holy Spirit, two, and the Holy Ghost, three, in the Bible, three ways of referring to the same Spirit. However, the Bible says Holy Ghost more than it does the Spirit of God or the Holy Spirit. Jesus said Holy Ghost most of the time and called his activity or movement the Comforter in John 14:26.

To take my analogy a step further, I can say the Holy Spirit is Trinitarian in the way he can be described. For example, it was revealed to me that the Holy Spirit is the breath of God, one, the voice of God, two, and the activity or movement of God, three, three ways of describing the same Spirit. I can go a step further and say the Holy Spirit is the lungs of God, one, the mouth of God, two, and the limbs of God, three. I can even break it down once more and say the Holy Spirit is the nose of God, one, the tongue of God, two, and the hands, feet, and bosom of God, three.

So, in summary, it was the Spirit of God whose voice made the world with his Word (Ps. 29:3-4), calling those things which be not as though they were (Rom. 4:17).

Again, it was the Spirit of God that formed mankind from the dust of the ground and breathed into his nostrils the breath of life and man became a living soul (Gen. 2:7).

It was the Spirit of God that called Noah and told him to build an ark of gopher wood (Gen. 6:14) big enough to house two animals and birds of every kind (Gen. 6:19-20). Then he shut the door (Gen. 7:16) with the animals and eight people inside and it rained forty days and forty nights without stopping (Gen. 7:17). But then the Spirit gave Noah the rainbow sign promising never again to destroy the earth with water (Gen. 9:12-16).

It was the Spirit of God that called Abraham and told him to leave his father's house and go to a place he would show him (Gen. 12:1-2). He told him he would be the father of many nations even though he was an old man married to an old woman with a barren womb (Gen. 15:5-6). Abraham believed the Spirit of God and it was counted to him for righteousness (Rom. 4:3). So when Abraham was a hundred years old (Gen. 21:5) and his wife Sarah was ninety years old, she gave birth to a son and called his name Isaac (Gen. 25-26) who was the father of Jacob whose name was changed to Israel (Gen. 32:28) who had twelve sons known as the twelve tribes of Israel (Gen. 35:22-26).

It was the Spirit of God that called Moses from a burning bush that was not consumed (Ex. 3:2) and told him to tell Pharaoh to "let my people go that they may worship me" (Ex. 4:23). The children of Israel spoiled Egypt taking gold, silver and precious stones (Ex. 12:35-36). Then the Spirit parted the Red Sea letting the Israelites walk through the sea on dry land (Ex. 14:21-22), but when Pharaoh's army followed behind he closed the sea back up and Pharaoh's army got drowned (Ex. 14: 23-29).

It was the Holy Spirit that sent Moses up on Mt. Sinai (Ex. 19:20) while the Holy Spirit wrote with his finger (Ex. 31:18) on tablets of stone (Ex. 24:12) The Ten Commandments he had spoken to his people (Ex. 20:1-17). Moses got angry with the people for worshipping a golden calf and he broke the first tablets and burned the calf in the fire (Ex. 32:19-20). So the Holy Spirit told Moses to make a second set of tablets and he would write again The Ten Commandments to be placed in a wooden ark (Deut. 10:1-4).

It was the Holy Spirit that called Joshua after Moses died and told him to take the children of Israel into the Promised Land (Josh. 1:1-2). The Holy Spirit told Joshua what battles to fight saying walk around Jericho one time for six days and on the seventh day walk around the city seven times behind seven priests with trumpets bearing the Ark of the Covenant. And on the seventh time blast the trumpets and lift up your voices and shout and I will make the walls of the city fall down (Josh. 6:1-5). So, "Joshua fit the battle of Jericho and the walls came tumbling down" (see Josh. 6:20).

It was the Holy Spirit that called the boy Samuel three times then came and stood calling him to be a prophet of his and a priest of Israel (1 Sam. 3:1-10). The Holy Spirit told Samuel to anoint David the shepherd boy from among his father Jesse's sons because one day he would be king of all Israel (1 Sam. 16:11-13).

It was the Holy Spirit that made David's son Solomon king after David died and told him to build a temple to house the Ark of the Covenant (1 Kings 5:5). It took seven years to build the temple (1 Kings 6:38) and when Solomon brought the Ark inside, the Holy Spirit filled the house in the form of a thick cloud (1 Kings 8:11).

It was the Holy Spirit that called all the prophets of God giving them supernatural power and miracles to perform. The prophet Elijah could run as fast

70

as a deer (1 Kings 18:46) and could hear the still small voice of God after the wind, earthquake and fire (1 Kings 19:12) and was taken up to heaven in a chariot of fire (2 Kings 2:11). The prophet Elisha raised the Shunammite woman's dead son (2 Kings 4:32-36) and made an axe head float (2 Kings 6:6). And, "In the year that King Uzziah died [the prophet Isaiah] saw the Lord sitting upon a throne, high and lifted up, and his train filled the temple" (Is. 6:1). The prophet Ezekiel saw "a wheel in the middle of a wheel" (Ez. 1:16). And in the prophet Daniel's book the Holy Spirit walked with the Hebrew boys in the burning fiery furnace (Dan. 3:24-25) and shut the mouths of hungry lions when Nebuchadnezzar, King of Babylon, had Daniel thrown in the lions' den (Dan. 6:22).

It was the Holy Ghost that put himself in the womb of a teenage virgin girl to take on human flesh and come into the world (Mt. 1:18).

It was the Holy Ghost that fed five thousand men plus women and children with five loaves of bread and two small fish (Mt. 14:14-21).

It was the Holy Ghost that gave sight to blind Bartimaeus who sat by the highway side begging (Mk. 10:46), and cleansed ten lepers even though only one came back to thank him (Lk. 17:11-18).

It was the Holy Ghost that healed the sick (Mk. 1:30-31), cast out demons (Lk. 8:26-35), walked on water (Mt. 14:25) and turned clear water into expensive white wine (Jn. 2:1-11).

It was the Holy Ghost that woke up Lazarus from the sleep of death lying dead in the tomb for four days. He came out, his hands and feet wrapped in grave clothes with a cloth around his face. The Holy Ghost told the people to "Loose him and let him go" (see Jn. 11:38-44).

It was the Holy Ghost that staggered up Golgatha hill and let the flesh part of himself be beaten and nailed to a cross to die for the sins of the world (Mt. 27:33-50).

It was the Holy Ghost that lay in the tomb and descended into hell to preach the gospel to the dead (2 Pet. 4:6), then got up on the third morning with all power in his hands (Mt. 28:18).

And, it is the Holy Ghost who is coming again to build the New Jerusalem with streets of gold (Rev. 21:21). There will be no more need for the sun because "the Lord God giveth them light" (Rev. 22:5), his own divine illumination, the same light in Genesis 1:3 shining four days before he even made the sun, and he is coming again to wipe all tears from our eyes (Rev. 21:4).

And, when he comes again, he will receive believers unto himself that where he is we may be also (Jn. 14:3).

It is high time we take the Holy Spirit whose name is Jesus from flesh back to Spirit in our mind's eye because of the resurrection.

CHAPTER 10

The Old Testament is not devoid of the Father's referring to the Son as God. Zechariah the prophet speaking for God says, "Awake, O sword, against my shepherd, against the man who is my companion, says the Lord of hosts" (Zech. 13:7). This verse causes me to reflect on Genesis 1:26 and 28 when God dialogues with himself about making human beings saying, "Let us make man in our image after our likeness" and making human beings telling them to be fruitful and multiply. God is about expanding his relationships with people.

Zechariah says in another place, "And I will pour upon the house of David, and upon the inhabitants of Jerusalem the spirit of grace and of supplication; and they shall look upon *me* whom they have pierced" (Zech. 12:10a) [emphasis mine]. The prophet is foretelling that God's flesh will one day be stabbed. Jesus was pierced in the side when he was crucified (see Jn. 19:34), the product of a hostile relationship on the part of humanity because of sin.

The New Testament supports the Old in conveying the certainty that Jesus is God and wants a relationship with his creation. The following is a passage written by the Apostle Paul that was given to me for my interpretation.

> Let this mind be in you which was also in Christ Jesus: Who being in the form of God, thought it not robbery to be equal with God: But made himself of no reputation, and took upon him the form of a servant, and was made in the likeness of men: And being found in fashion as a man, humbled himself, and became obedient unto death, even the death of the cross. Wherefore [he is] highly exalted and [has] a name which is above every name: That at the name of Jesus every knee should bow, of things in heaven, and things in earth, and things under the earth; And that every tongue should confess that Jesus Christ is [the Lord of glory]. (Phil. 2:5-11)

Jesus refers to himself as God to the Jews who were asking for a sign to show them how he had the nerve to do and say what he did. Jesus was in Jerusalem at Passover and he had already driven the moneychangers out of the temple. He said to the Jews, "Destroy this temple and in three days I will raise it up" (Jn. 2:19), referring to his dead body but they thought he was talking about the temple building. Jesus did not say the Father would raise him up because they are one and the same. He said he would raise himself.

Jesus expresses how he values the action part of himself when he says blaspheming the Holy Ghost is a sin that cannot be forgiven (see Mt. 12:32). That is understandable because Jesus was only a man for thirty-three or so years. What is that compared to eternity? And the creative energy of the Holy Ghost was released when God spoke, that acted on his words benefiting more than just himself. In other words, Jesus does what he says because he loves his creation and is not a man that he should lie (Num. 23:19). Because of his loving attitude toward us, the world is blessed.

Jesus says, "Believest thou not that I am in the Father, and the Father in me? the words that I speak unto you I speak not of myself: but the Father that dwelleth in me, he doeth the works. Believe me that I am in the Father, and the Father in me: or else believe me for the very works sake" (Jn. 14:10-11). Jesus is saying who he is—that he is God—without the sensationalism and to keep from sounding like he is bragging.

Revelation 7:17 says, "And the lamb which is in the *midst of the throne* [emphasis mine] shall feed them, and shall lead them unto living fountains of water: and God shall wipe away all tears from their eyes." The main point here is that Jesus is in the middle of the throne and there is only one throne. Sitting at the right hand of the Father does not mean two people sitting or standing side-by-side, one being superior to the other, but one God moving or circulating in the center of whatever the throne is. He wipes tears from our eyes because of his loving attitude toward us.

When Jesus says, "The Father is greater than I" (Jn. 14:28), he is referring to that part of himself that never condescended to put on flesh, his original thoughts that stayed in heaven because the world was too small to hold them. God's thoughts are analogous to John 21:25 where the gospel writer says, "And there are also many other things which Jesus did, the which, if they should be written every one, I suppose that even the world itself could not contain the books that should be written." He does all things for us out of his great love.

John says that Jesus Christ is the true God and eternal life (see 1 Jn. 5:20). Peter says Jesus "was foreordained before the foundation of the world, but was manifest in these last times for you" (1 Pet. 1:20). And Paul says, "that God was in Christ, reconciling the world unto himself" (2 Cor. 5:19).

Further support that Jesus is God is in verses that speak of God as our Savior such as "For this is good and acceptable in the sight of God our Savior" (1 Tim. 2:3). "Therefore we both labor and suffer reproach, because we trust in the living God, who is the Savior of all men, especially of those that believe" (1 Tim. 4:10). We are "looking for that blessed hope, and the glorious appearing of our great God and our Savior Jesus Christ" (Titus 2:13).

I substituted the verb "is" for the pronoun "he" in the following verse to give my interpretation. "But after that the kindness and love of God our Savior toward man appeared, Not by works of righteousness which we have done, but according to his mercy he saved us, by the washing of regeneration, and renewing of the Holy Ghost; which [is] shed on us abundantly through Jesus Christ our Savior" (Titus 3:4-6).

And, this verse fits what Jesus called me to do. "In hope of eternal life, which God, that cannot lie, promised before the world began; But hath in due times manifested his word through preaching, which is committed unto me according to the commandment of God our Savior" (Titus 1:3).

The last of the "God our Savior" verses I am using is a straightforward benediction. "To the only wise God our Savior, be glory and majesty, dominion and power, both now and ever. Amen" (Jude 25).

CHAPTER 11

I thought it would be helpful at this time to share the very first Bible verses given to me that I started writing down many years ago and have been adding to up until now. The Spirit said I could put in brackets my new interpretations where needed.

The first verses are warnings of Jesus. "Whosoever, therefore, shall be ashamed of me in this adulterous and sinful generation, of him also shall [I] be ashamed, when [I] come in [my] glory ... with the holy angels" (Mk. 8:38).

"Wherefore, behold, I send unto you prophets, and wise men, and scribes; and some of them ye shall kill and crucify, and some of them shall ye scourge in your synagogues, and persecute them from city to city" (Mt. 23:34). But understand, "He that is not with me is against me; and he that gathereth not with me scattereth abroad" (Mt. 12:30).

"Take heed to yourselves; for they shall deliver you up to councils, and in the synagogues ye shall be beaten; and ye shall be brought before rulers and kings for my sake, for a testimony against them. And the gospel must first be proclaimed among all nations. But when they shall lead you, and deliver you up, take no thought beforehand what ye shall speak, neither do ye premeditate; but whatsoever shall be given you in that hour, that speak ye; for it is not ye that speak, but [my] Holy Spirit. ... And ye shall be hated of all men for my name's sake; but he that shall endure to the end, the same shall be saved" (Mk. 13:9-11, 13).

"These things have I spoken unto you, that ye should not be offended. They shall put you out of the synagogues.... And these things will they do unto you, because they have not known ... me. But these things have I told you, that when the time shall come, ye may remember that I told you of them" (Jn. 16:1-4). So "Gird up thy loins and arise and speak unto them all that I command thee: be not dismayed at their faces, lest I confound thee before them" (Jer. 1:17).

Jesus said to the Jews, "Search the scriptures; for in them ye think ye have eternal life: and they are they which testify of me" (Jn. 5:39), and he told me to continue to search the Scriptures saying, "Behold, I have set before you an open door, which no one is able to shut; I know that you have but little power, and yet you have kept my word and have not denied my name" (Rev. 3:8).

"Abide in me, and I in you. As the branch cannot bear fruit of itself, except it abide in the vine; no more can ye, except ye abide in me" (Jn. 15:4). "He that abideth in me, and I in him, the same bringeth forth much fruit" (Jn. 15:5). "If ye abide in me, and my words abide in you, ye shall ask what ye will, and it shall be done unto you" (Jn. 15:7). "If ye keep my commandments, ye shall abide in my love; even as I have kept my ... [Word] and abide in [eternal] love" (Jn. 15:10).

"What I tell you in darkness, that speak ye in light: and what ye hear in the ear, that preach ye upon the housetops" (Mt. 10:27). That verse is the foundation of my prayer ministry. "And I will give thee the treasures of darkness, and hidden riches of secret places, that thou mayest know that I, the Lord, which call thee by thy name, am the God of Israel" (Is. 45:3). "Go into all the world and preach the gospel to every creature. He that believeth and is baptized shall be saved; but he that believeth not shall be damned" (Mk. 16:15). "I, even I, am he that blotteth out thy transgressions for mine own sake, and will not remember thy sins" (Is. 43:25).

When I was having a hard time in another denomination during the early stages of my ministry for putting emphasis on Jesus as the embodiment of the Trinity, the Spirit led me to these verses. "Blessed are you when men hate you, and when they exclude you, and revile you, and cast out your name as evil, for the Son of Man's sake" (Lk. 6:22). "Verily, verily, I say unto you, That ye shall weep and lament, but the world shall rejoice and ye shall be sorrowful, but your sorrow shall turn into joy" (Jn. 16:20). "Be of good cheer; it is I; be not afraid" (Mt. 14:27). "Behold, I give you authority to tread on serpents and scorpions and over all the power of the enemy, and nothing shall by any means hurt you" (Lk. 10:19). "Be not afraid, only believe" (Mk. 5:36).

The following verses are the foundation of my pulpit ministry. "I, if I be lifted up from the earth, will draw all [people] unto me" (Jn. 12:32). "I am the resurrection and the life" (Jn. 11:25). And "I am the way; follow me" (Jn. 14:6; 12:26).

The Apostle Paul says that "God [has] made foolish the wisdom of this world For after that in the wisdom of God the world by wisdom knew not God, it pleased God by the foolishness of preaching to save them that believe" (1 Cor. 1:20b-21). The Apostle Peter says that Jesus even descended into hell to preach the gospel to the dead. "For this cause was the gospel preached also to them that are dead, that they might be judged according to men in the flesh, but live according to God in the spirit" (1 Pet. 4:6). And when Jesus walked the earth he said to his disciples, "I must preach the kingdom of God to other cities also: for therefore [did I come here]" (Lk. 4:43). I too must preach and share the Bible verses given to me.

The Spirit said, "Follow me" (Mk. 2:14) and "[You] shall be taught [by me]" (Jn. 6:45). "Be of good cheer; it is I; be not afraid" (Mk. 6:50). He had to tell me that more than once. For "All things are possible to [her] that believes" (Mk. 9:23).

"Whoever hears you hears me, and whoever rejects you rejects me" (Lk. 10:16). "Verily I say unto you, There be some of them that stand here, who shall not taste of death, till they have seen the kingdom of God come with power" (Mk. 9:1).

When I was under spiritual attack and could not seem to shake the fear of death, the Spirit led me to this verse: "He that findeth his life shall lose it: and he that loseth his life for my sake shall find it" (Mt. 10:39).

Regarding the devil he says, "How can one enter into a strong man's house, and spoil his goods, except he first bind the strong man? and then he will spoil his house" (Mt. 12:29). "When the enemy shall come in like a flood, the

Spirit of the Lord shall lift up a standard against him" (Is. 59:19b). "Why do you not judge for [yourself] what is right?" (Lk. 12:57). So I come against Satan immediately when he is trying to get a foothold to stop him from getting a stronghold. Jesus even said, "Get thee behind me, Satan" (Mk. 8:33). And he said when casting out a demon, "I order you to come out" (Mk. 9:25). I must do the same in the name of Jesus, of course, since Jesus is the only name the devil fears.

Fighting principalities and powers, I often had to refer to verses in the Book of Revelation like, "Now is come salvation, and strength, and the kingdom of our God, and the power of … Christ: for the accuser of our brethren is cast down" (Rev. 12:10). "They overcame him by the blood of the Lamb, and by the word of their testimony" (Rev. 12:11a).

When I get physically and mentally tired, I read these verses: "In returning and rest shall ye be saved; in quietness and in confidence shall be your strength" (Is. 30:15). "To you who are troubled rest with us, when the Lord Jesus shall be revealed from heaven with his mighty angels" (2 Thes. 1:7). "And he said unto them, Come ye yourselves apart into a desert place, and rest a while: for there [will be] many coming and going, and [you will have] no leisure so much as to eat" (Mk. 6:31). This tells me that my preaching engagements will be increasing.

In closing this chapter of "More personal verses" Jesus says, "I will put upon you none other burden. But that which ye have already hold fast till I come" (Rev. 2:24b-25). "Hitherto have you asked nothing in My name: ask, and you shall receive, that your joy may be full" (Jn. 16:24). "Worship God: for the testimony of Jesus is the spirit of prophecy" (Rev. 19:10).

When Christ comes again, his name will no longer be Jesus. Then "His name is called The Word of God" (Rev. 19:13).

The Spirit said to me, "If you know [certain] things, happy are you if you do them" (Jn. 13:17) for "I will utter things [to you] which have been kept secret from the foundation of the world" (Mt. 13:35). "[I am glad that I have] hid these

things from the wise and prudent, and hast revealed them unto babes. Even so …
for it seemed good in [my] sight" (Mt. 11:25).

"No man can serve two masters: for either he will hate the one, and love
the other; or else he will hold to the one, and despise the other" (Mt. 6:24). Here
Jesus is saying that he is the one true God. "Who has an ear, let him hear what
the Spirit says" (Rev. 2:7).

CHAPTER 12

At the end of writing my memoir it was revealed to me that I should be "confident of this very thing, that he who has begun a good work in [me] will carry it on to completion until the day of Jesus Christ" (Phil. 1:6). But then like David I asked, "Who am I, O Lord Jehovah, and what is my house, that you have brought me thus far?" (2 Sam. 7:18).

The Spirit said obedient people will be rewarded. "They shall call them, the holy people, The redeemed of the Lord: and thou shalt be called, Sought out, A city not forsaken" (Is. 62:11-12) for "[People] took knowledge of them, that they had been with Jesus" (Acts 4:13). This was a humbling experience for me comparable to when I was called to preach the gospel.

Many verses in the Bible have hidden meanings because initially the gospel message was hard to hear. For example, Jesus told the Jews that he is the bread which came down from heaven, and they murmured about that (see Jn. 6:41). Even some of his disciples did not like his saying, "Except ye eat the flesh of the Son of man, and drink his blood, ye have no life in you" (Jn. 6:53). Many said, "This is an hard saying; who can hear it?" (Jn. 6:60) and left him. "Then Jesus said unto the twelve, Will ye also go away? Then Simon Peter answered him, Lord, to whom shall we go? thou hast the words of eternal life" (Jn. 6:67-68), and he was right.

I was also given these verses: "Whatsoever thy hand findeth to do, do it with thy might" (Eccl. 9:10) and "Do all that is in thine heart; for [I am] with you" (1 Chron. 17:2). When I asked "Why me?" he led me to 1 Corinthians 1:27-28 that says, "[I have] chosen the foolish things of the world to confound the wise; … the weak things of the world to confound the things which are mighty; And base things of the world, and things which are despised, [have I] chosen, yea, and things which are not, to bring to naught things that are." Therefore, I accepted my assignment and stepped out on faith.

So a summary of my memoir is a familiar phrase stated in Communion services in Methodist churches that describes the Godhead. That phrase is "thought, Word, and deed." Thought is God the Father, Word is God the Son and deed is God the Holy Spirit. God the Father is original thought supported in Isaiah 14:24, God the Son is the articulated Word supported in John 1:1-3 and 14, and God the Holy Spirit is deed supported in Genesis 1:1-2. The phrase can also be explained this way with parts of Scripture: Thought—"Surely as I have thought" (Is. 14:24a). Word—"And God said" (Gen. 1:3). Deed—"And it was so" (Gen. 1:7). The person of God is Jesus of Nazareth, the Christ. "His name shall be called Wonderful, Counselor, The mighty God, The everlasting Father, The Prince of Peace" (Is. 9:6) and in the world to come The Word of God (see Rev. 19:13).

Jesus is the articulation of divine thought as well as the flesh of God. As soon as God spoke his thoughts, at the same time what God said happened, indicating that the spoken word is the activity or movement of God called the Holy Spirit or Holy Ghost.

At creation God thought, God spoke, and God acted. That is how God is Three in One. God thinks, speaks and acts all at the same time. So a way of describing the Trinity, meaning God the Father, Son, and Holy Ghost, is "thought, Word, and deed." That is also a way of explaining how human beings are created in the image of God because we too can think, speak, and act.

The name of God is Jesus, which means Savior. "You shall call his name JESUS: for he shall save his people from their sins" (Mt. 1:21).

God decided to put on flesh and come to earth—known as the incarnation—and when he did he "went about doing good" (Acts 10:38), but he angered high officials with his teachings and miracles. Because they were jealous of him (see Mk. 15:10), he was falsely accused (Mk. 15:3), tried and sentenced to death by crucifixion under Pontius Pilate (Mk. 15:15). Jesus died on a cross (Mk. 15:37) and was buried in Joseph of Arimathea's new tomb (Mk. 15:46). On the third morning Jesus rose from the dead (Mk. 16:2) with all power in heaven and on earth (Mt. 28:18). That says to me that Jesus took himself from flesh back to Spirit after the resurrection and so should we.

When Jesus died on the cross and rose from the dead he went back to the eternal part of himself, his thoughts. His flesh called the Son died for the sins of the world (Jn. 3:16) and he descended into hell to preach the gospel to the dead (1 Pet. 4:6). Again, every time we read "Son of God" in the Bible, we should think "Flesh of God," because it was revealed to me that "Son" means "Flesh."

Before he died on the cross Jesus said, "I am the light of the world" (Jn. 8:12). He rose from the dead fulfilling the prophecy of Isaiah: "Arise, shine; for thy light is come, and the glory of the Lord is risen upon thee" (Is. 60:1). The sun rises to give light to the world; Jesus rises for the salvation of the world.

Again, the incarnated Jesus was fully God and fully man, but the resurrected Jesus has all power in heaven and on earth (Mt. 28:18). God is "thought, Word, and deed" whose name is Jesus. Scripture interprets Scripture and the Holy Ghost explains himself; so my main job when writing this book was not to interfere with him. "The Sovereign Lord has sworn by himself—the Lord God Almighty declares" (Amos 6:8) this. And the main revelation the Holy Ghost gave me is God the Father is the Pre-incarnate Christ, meaning Jesus before he was born of The Virgin Mary. The Spirit said he reserved this word for me.

Now that I am finished I can relate to the psalmist who says, "You, Lord, have made me glad through Your work: I will triumph in the works of Your hands" (Ps. 92:4) for "It is God which works in [me] both to will and to do his good pleasure" (Phil. 2:13). "I pray always for myself that God would count me worthy of his calling and fulfill all the good pleasure of his goodness, and the work of faith with power (2 Thes. 1:11). "He that testifieth these things saith, Surely I come quickly. Amen. Even so, come, Lord Jesus" (Rev. 22:20).

CHAPTER 13

I have written a sermon for the last chapter because the Word says, "It pleased God by the foolishness of preaching to save them that believe" (1 Cor. 1:21b).

2 Chronicles 6:12-21

1 Corinthians 1:17-24

Luke 11:29-31

JESUS: THE GOD OF POWER AND WISDOM

Our Old Testament text, 2 Chronicles 6:12-21, is about King Solomon's prayer that he prayed when dedicating the temple he built in Jerusalem. It's almost verbatim to 1 Kings 8:22-30 except here a different version is given for how he prayed. First Kings 8:22 says, "Solomon stood before the altar of the Lord in the presence of all the congregation of Israel, and spread forth his hands toward heaven."

Second Chronicles 6:12, our Scripture for today says, "He stood before the altar of the Lord in the presence of all the congregation of Israel, and spread forth his hands." So first some background on how King Solomon got to this point.

As you know, Solomon was the son of David and you know about David. He was the shepherd boy who killed a Philistine giant with his slingshot and a stone (1 Sam. 13:17:49-50). He grew up and was chosen by God from all of his father Jesse's sons to be anointed by the prophet Samuel (1 Sam. 16:11-13). David later became king after the death of Saul, Israel's first king (2 Sam. 5:4-5).

David was a man after God's own heart (see 1 Sam. 13-14) because he called on the name of the Lord often. Even when he was wrong he prayed confessing his sins. But most of his prayers were songs of praise like many of the Psalms he wrote. David was a man of prayer and so was Solomon, initially.

84

Bathsheba was Solomon's mother, Uriah the Hittite's wife. David impregnated Bathsheba and had Uriah killed so he could marry her. David had Joab, his commander-in-chief (Bryant 284), put Uriah in the forefront of the hottest battle and withdraw his soldiers so that he would be slain (2 Sam. 11:14-17). This displeased the Lord very much and God had Nathan the prophet tell him so (2 Sam. 12:1-14). The first child David and Bathsheba had died (2 Sam. 12:15-18) but God forgave them for their adultery. We know this because their next child was Solomon and the Word says God loved him. Solomon was also named Jedidiah, which means "beloved of the Lord" (2 Sam. 12:24-25) (Bryant 560). David and Bathsheba had four children together (1 Chron. 3:5).

Solomon became king after his father David, but Scripture presents David as the best king although Solomon accumulated great wealth during the forty years he reigned over all Israel (Zodhiates 455).

Solomon asked God for wisdom. The Word says the Lord appeared to him in a dream and told him to ask for what he wanted and Solomon said, "Give … thy servant an understanding heart to judge thy people, that I may discern between good and bad" (1 Kin. 3:9). Well the Lord was pleased with his answer and told him because he didn't ask for long life or riches or the death of his enemies but asked for understanding, he would give him that plus riches and honor too. God even told him that nobody before or after would ever be like him and no other king would equal him as long as he lived (see 1 Kin. 3:3-13).

A famous story about Solomon has to do with two prostitutes who lived together. They gave birth about the same time and both had sons. One smothered her baby by accident when she was asleep and when she realized what she had done she switched her dead baby with the other woman's live baby. But the live baby's mother knew what had happened and went and told King Solomon. He heard them both lay claim to the live baby and told one of his soldiers to take his sword and split the baby in half, that way both would have him. The woman who switched the babies said kill him but the real mother was willing to give her baby to the woman just to keep him alive. So Solomon gave her the baby knowing she was the child's mother. People who witnessed what he did knew he had the wisdom of God (1 Kin. 3:16-28).

In the fourth year of Solomon's reign as king of Israel, after his father David, Solomon began to build the temple in Jerusalem (see 1 Kin. 6:1). David wanted to build the temple but God told him no because he had shed so much blood (1 Chron. 22:8) being a warrior. God told him, "Your son Solomon will build me a house because he will be a man of peace and I will give him rest from war" (1 Chron. 22:9-10).

David accepted what God said and made provisions to help Solomon build the temple. He gave him tons of gold, silver, iron, brass, and copper. He left massive stones for the foundation of the building, loads of cedar for the walls and roof, bolts of silk and other cloth for the veil and to wrap the utensils, cups and bowls as well as chests of precious jewels like rubies and pearls, the spoils of war.

David was rich from the treasures he took from the countries he conquered. And before he died, David commanded the princes of Israel to help Solomon, reminding them of his tender age—he was only about nineteen at the time—and the peace they would enjoy during his reign (1 Chron. 22:5), 14, 16, and 18).

So after David died and Solomon because king, he began construction on the temple that would take seven years to complete. But it was while the temple was being built that something wonderful happened. God appeared to Solomon and spoke to him. God said, "Concerning this house you are building, if you will walk in my statutes, execute my judgments and keep all my commandments to walk in them, I will do what I promised David your father. I will live among the children of Israel and not forget them" (1 Kin. 6:11-13).

And that's what was wonderful! Solomon heard the voice of the Lord— which is Jesus—as clearly as you hear mine. God said to him, "If you keep my commandments, I will live with you and keep you on my mind." That means he would personally be with Israel and think about them all the time. So the Word says, "Solomon built the house and finished it" (1 Kin. 6:11-14).

The start of 1 Kings 8 tells about how Solomon set up the dedication service. He assembled the elders of Israel, the heads of the tribes and the chief fathers—all the big shots—in the temple so he could bring up the ark out of the City of David to the temple, because that's why it was built. In other words, they took the Ark of the Covenant that was kept in a tent and brought it to a building, the temple.

The ark was basically a rectangular box inlayed with pure gold inside and out (see Ex. 25:10-16). Inside it were the tablets with The Ten Commandments written on them, the golden pot that had manna from heaven that God gave the Israelites to eat when they journeyed in the wilderness, and Aaron's rod that bloomed (Heb. 9:4) although 1 Kings 8:9 says, "There was nothing in the ark save the two tables of stone, which Moses put there at Horeb."

The Ark of the Covenant represented the presence of God in the midst of Israel, and it could not be touched. Only the priests could handle it and they had to take up the ark with wooden poles that were put through rings on each end and carry it on their shoulders. So Solomon had them bring the ark before the congregation assembled in the temple and it was done in grand fashion. The priests sacrificed sheep and oxen and then set up the Ark in the holy place, poles and all (1 Kin. 8:8).

But the highlight of the whole event was what God did. The Word says, "It came to pass, when the priests were come out of the holy place, that a cloud filled the house of the Lord so that the priests could not stand to minister because of the cloud: for the glory of the Lord had filled the house of the Lord" (1 Kin. 8:10-11).

What happened was God manifested himself. He personally came on the scene. The cloud was the Pre-Incarnate Christ. In other words, the cloud was Jesus and the voice was Jesus. He showed up in person to let everybody know that he was keeping his promise to David. And that's why Solomon couldn't help doing what he did. He stood up and prayed. He lifted his hands, looked toward heaven and called on the name of the Lord.

Now our text this morning, 2 Chronicles 6:13, adds that "Solomon had made a brazen [which means brass] scaffold, five cubits long [that's 7 ½ feet], five cubits broad, and three cubits high [that's a little over 4 feet], and had set it in the midst of the court: and upon it he stood, and kneeled down upon his knees before all the congregation of Israel, and spread forth his hands toward heaven." Then he prayed out loud.

The prayer in 2 Chronicles 6 is practically identical to the one in 1 Kings 8. But one of the main points I'm making is that Solomon had sense enough to pray in the first place, to call on the name of the Lord because prayer is the foundation of all ministry. What we do when we pray is acknowledge the power and wisdom of God, who God is, what God has done, what God is doing, what God will do.

The Word says, "The Lord by wisdom founded the earth" (Prov. 3:19) and "Wisdom abides in the [person] of understanding" (Prov. 14:33). But I'm particularly intrigued with King Solomon, the man God singled out to bless with wisdom, riches and fame. We read that "God gave Solomon wisdom and understanding beyond measure and largeness of heart" (1 Kin. 4:29).

Solomon was aware of God's generosity to him, which he expressed in his prayer before the assembly. On his knees with his hands spread toward heaven he prayed, "O Lord God of Israel, there is no God like thee in heaven, nor in the earth; which keepest covenant, and shewest mercy unto thy servants, that walk before thee with all their hearts" (2 Chron. 6:14). He proceeds to ask God to remember his people in war, famine and sorrow and to remember the temple and his father David.

God's response is, "If my people, which are called by my name, shall humble themselves, and pray, and seek my face, and turn from their wicked ways; then will I hear from heaven, and will forgive their sin, and will heal their land" (2 Chron. 7:14).

But the main thing that became clear to me from the dialogue between Solomon and God is this: God has a voice we can hear too and the voice of God is Jesus, which is power and wisdom. Exodus 19:19 says, "When the voice of the trumpet sounded long, and waxed louder and louder, Moses spake, and God answered him by a voice." Jesus says in John 10:27, "My sheep hear my voice and I know them and they follow me."

Solomon wrote about the wisdom of God saying, "Wisdom is the principle thing, therefore get wisdom: and with all thy getting get understanding" (Prov. 4:17) for "Happy is the [person] that finds wisdom and ... understanding" (Prov. 3:13). He says, wisdom is better than rubies; and all the things that may be desired are not to be compared to it" (Prov. 8:11).

"Wisdom is of more value than foolishness, just as light is better than darkness; for the wise [person] sees while the fool is blind" (Eccl. 2:13). Speaking from experience, no doubt, he says, "To be wise is as good as being rich; in fact, it is better" (Eccl. 7:11).

So we see that Solomon had a lot of information about wisdom that the Holy Ghost gave him because he was able to hear the voice of the Lord. And we see that whatever God speaks is power and wisdom.

The wisdom of God was also made audible to others in the Bible. Job says, "Behold, the fear of the Lord, that is wisdom; and to depart from evil is understanding" (Job 28:28). The psalmist phrases it this way: "The fear of the Lord is the beginning of wisdom" (Ps. 111:10). Here we see that the writers are not talking about wisdom so much as defining it. Both say that wisdom is fear of the Lord.

But isn't God defined as love (see Rom. 8:39) and light (Jn. 8:12)? Are we supposed to be afraid of who comforts us and enables us to understand things? Evidently we are because God is also described as a "consuming fire" (Heb. 12:29) and even refers to himself as "a jealous God" (Ex. 30:5). So it follows that we must fear the Lord if we want to have wisdom.

However, for some of us it's hard to see how shaking in our shoes at God would make us wise. There must be something more to the word fear than being scared and there is.

A dictionary definition of fear is awe and reverence, deep respect for something. That means the key to understanding what wisdom is and how it works is having respect. In order to gain the wisdom of God, respect is what we need most. At any age the beginning of wisdom occurs when we learn the meaning of respect.

In my opinion, respect is an attitude; it's the way we think about something or someone. We learn respect in the home. The first people we usually respect are our parents. One of The Ten Commandments is, "Honor thy father and thy mother that things may go well with you and that your days will be long in the land" (Ex. 20:12).

Respect is doing what's right. It's realizing that how we act is important. The Word says, "We must work out our own salvation with fear and trembling" (Phil. 2:12) because "We all must stand before the judgment seat of Christ" (Rom. 14:10).

Respect is having principles below what we will not go and involves paying attention to our conscience. We all have one. It's a manifestation of God in all people—the still small voice of God, if you will. But we don't always listen to our conscience. Sometimes we don't trust it or we ignore it. Some don't believe the conscience is God's voice telling them the right thing to do. Or if they do believe they tell themselves God is so merciful he won't unleash punishment.

Some act like they don't have a conscience and never had one, being headstrong and willful. But what's interesting is if we go ahead and do something wrong, we still know it's wrong and we're not comfortable about it either. Wrongdoing makes most of us nervous, which brings me back to the subject of fear and the part it plays in wisdom.

Fearing the Lord has to do with knowing the truth. The truth is we're afraid of what we can't control, which includes many things. For example, we can't do a thing with the elements. A rainstorm can come and flood shorelines and basements and all we can do is pump the water out and wait.

A snowstorm can close schools and shut down a city. All we can do is shovel our sidewalks and driveways and hope we don't fall down or have a car accident.

When a tornado hits, all we can do is run and hide. Modern terminology calls it taking shelter, but it boils down to hiding from the movement of God.

When an earthquake strikes, all we can do is be amazed at what's taking place. The earth actually moves and cracks open. All we can do when that happens is wonder how long it will last because the ground's moving for any length of time wreaks havoc. Imagine if earthquakes lasted for more than a few seconds. Everything would collapse and get swallowed up. And we can't do a thing about it.

What we have absolutely no control of—which is most things—makes us rightfully afraid and very aware of our limitations. What we do have some control of is ourselves, but sometimes even that's questionable.

However, when we allow ourselves to be convinced that the voice of the Lord, Jesus, made the world and everything in it—including us—wisdom begins. Acknowledging that the Triune God of heaven and earth—Jesus—is to be respected, indicates the presence of wisdom.

As children, we fear things like the dark and loud noises. We usually fear our parents because they discipline us and we depend on them for everything up to a certain age.

We need to fear some people like our teachers, because they've been put in charge of our minds. They influence the way we think about the world and ourselves.

We fear the police because they can take us to jail or prison and take away our freedom. They can fine us and take away our money. And sometimes they can even take away our life. Solomon says, "Young men who are wise obey the law. A son who is a member of a lawless gang is a shame to his [parents]" (Prov. 28:7). Of course that applies to girls too. Some things need to be feared.

91

We should fear ourselves to a certain extent because we can do ourselves harm. Our emotions are tied up in our immune system and influence it. We can feel guilty about something and make ourselves so depressed we get sick. Our thoughts can make us physically and mentally ill.

For example, we can worry and develop stomach ulcers. We can hate someone so much that we can cause our own minds to deteriorate. We can actually run ourselves crazy hating and trying to get revenge.

And we can make ourselves sick with regrets, saying I wish I had done this or I wish I hadn't done that. Sickness brought on by the mind is proof that we can endanger ourselves by the way we think. Solomon says in Proverbs 23:7, "As [a man] thinketh in his heart, so is he." He also says in Proverbs 4:23, "Be careful how you think; your life is shaped by your thoughts" (TEV).

We can see how respect and fear are interchangeable. Fear is having respect. To fear the Lord is to respect what God can do. Jesus tells us not to fear people who can kill the body but afterwards can't do anything more. He says, "Fear God who, after killing, has the power to throw into hell" (Mt. 10:12), talking about himself, of course. He is the one who can literally make us shake in our shoes. But what does God do? He has mercy on us.

God asks the question, "Can anyone hide from me? Am I not everywhere in all of heaven and earth?" (Jer. 23:24). That's where Solomon's behavior in his later years is hard to understand. As you know, he married many foreign women and ended up worshiping their gods (Bryant 560). He broke the first commandment. God says, "I am the Lord thy God, which have brought thee out of the land of Egypt, out of the house of bondage. Thou shalt have no other gods before me. … Thou shalt not bow down thyself to them, nor serve them: for I the Lord thy God am a jealous God, visiting the iniquity of the fathers upon the children unto the third and fourth generation of them that hate me; and showing mercy unto thousands of them that love me, and keep my commandments" (Ex. 20:2-3, 5-6).

Solomon knowingly disobeyed God. He had the Law of Moses to go by but what really caused him to have no excuse is God appeared to him twice: in Gibeon in a dream (1 Kin. 3:5) and by night after the temple dedication (2 Chron. 7:12). The God of heaven and earth spoke to Solomon on two separate occasions (Bryant 560), yet he ended up acting like hearing God's voice was no big deal. Solomon will go down in history as a wise and knowledgeable man who didn't practice what he preached.

Jesus reflected on him when rebuking the Pharisees for seeking a sign before they would believe saying, "The queen of the south shall rise up in the judgment with this generation, and shall condemn it: for she came from the uttermost parts of the earth to hear the wisdom of Solomon; and, behold, a greater than Solomon is here" (Mt. 12:42).

I'm reminded of my maternal grandfather, James William McKinley Carr. He used to talk about people who had gone to college but had no common sense. He said, "An educated fool is an abomination," and he could make abomination sound like a cuss word.

From King Solomon I learned that wisdom, although wonderful to have, is not enough. We need a Savior. People can't save themselves no matter how wise, rich or famous they may be. We're not able to resist temptation on our own. We sin in spite of our good intentions. Grace has to intercede and help us.

We need to "pray without ceasing" (1 Thes. 5:17) for the Holy Spirit to guide and instruct us. We need to hear and obey the voice of the Lord so we won't "run this race in vain" (see Heb. 12:1).

A wise person believes that Jesus is Lord and Savior, the only wisdom that does any of us any good.

Jesus is the Father's flesh, "the true God and eternal life" (1 Jn. 5:20).

Works Cited

African Methodist Episcopal Church Hymnal.   Nashville: The African
    Methodist Episcopal Church, 2000.

Bryant, T. Alton, ed. The New Compact Bible Dictionary. Grand Rapids:
    Zondervan, 1967.

Dake, Finis Jennings. Dake's Annotated Reference Bible. Lawrenceville,
    GA: Dake, 2001.

Foster, Richard J. Prayer: Finding the Heart's True Home. San Francisco:
    Harper, 1992.

Holy Bible: New International Version. Colorado Springs: International
    Bible Society, 1984.

Holy Bible: Revised Standard Version. New York: Collins' Clear-Type,
    1952.

Marshall, Anita. "God's People Restored Again." The Improved Adult
    Teacher Church School Quarterly: Spring Quarter, March, April, May.
    Nashville: The African Methodist Episcopal Church, 2009.

Strong, James. Strong's Exhaustive Concordance of the Bible. Iowa Falls:
    World, 1986.

Thompson, Frank Charles. The Thompson Chain-Reference Bible. 5th ed.
    Indianapolis: B. B. Kirkbride, 1988.

Wright, Jr., R. R., and John R. Hawkins, eds. Encyclopaedia of African
    Methodism. Vol. 1. Philadelphia: R. R. Wright, Jr., 1916.

Zodhiates, Spiros, ed. Hebrew-Greek Key Word Study Bible: King James
    Version. Chattanooga: AMG, 1991.